With Peter to Calvary

The elders which are among you I exhort, who am also an elder, and a witness of the sufferings of Christ.

1 Peter 5[1]

With Peter to Calvary

GOOD FRIDAY TALKS

by

S. Val Green

LONDON : THE EPWORTH PRESS

THE EPWORTH PRESS
(FRANK H. CUMBERS)
25-35, City Road, London, E.C.1

MELBOURNE   CAPE TOWN
NEW YORK   TORONTO

SET IN MONOTYPE BASKERVILLE AND PRINTED IN
GREAT BRITAIN BY THE CAMELOT PRESS LTD.,
LONDON AND SOUTHAMPTON

For My Wife

PREFACE

THE SUBJECT of this book has been treated by many authors in many different ways. It has been approached from so many different angles that only some new method could hope to gain for it that quota of readers that would make the book worth while.

I have had two purposes in writing it.

First, as one who for many years has had to take his own Three Hours' Service on Good Friday, I have had in mind those who either through the remoteness of their churches, or the difficulty of obtaining a preacher who could efficiently tackle the task which this great service imposes, have had to do the same. To them this ever-recurring service often brings difficulties. What can they say that they have not already said many times? How can they bring new interest to their people; new light on the Divine Tragedy? It is not my suggestion that they should use the following chapters as addresses as they stand, but it is my hope that they will find an occasional new idea, and at least a fresh presentation.

My second purpose has been to provide for those who either through ill-health or the lack of local facility are unable to attend a Three Hours' Service on Good Friday. They, I hope, will find in the following pages that which will help them to watch by the Cross, and to see in that drama much more than appears from a surface reading of the New Testament account.

My grateful thanks are due to the Archdeacon of Durham, the Venerable E. de Grey Lucas, who has kindly read through and corrected the typescript, and who gave me many useful suggestions for the final revision, and also to Dr Coggan for his careful vetting of the whole work and his impartial Foreword.

S. V. G.

CONTENTS

PREFACE 7

FOREWORD 11

1. 'THE LORD TURNED AND LOOKED UPON PETER' . 13

2. 'FATHER, FORGIVE THEM; FOR THEY KNOW NOT
   WHAT THEY DO' 25

3. 'TODAY SHALT THOU BE WITH ME IN PARADISE' . 41

4. 'WOMAN, BEHOLD THY SON; SON, BEHOLD THY
   MOTHER' 55

5. 'MY GOD, MY GOD, WHY HAST THOU FORSAKEN
   ME?' 71

6. 'I THIRST' 84

7. 'IT IS FINISHED' 97

8. 'FATHER, INTO THY HANDS I COMMEND MY SPIRIT' 108

FOREWORD

IN HIS Preface to the most recent edition of Dr James Denney's *The Death of Christ*, Professor R. V. G. Tasker reminds us of a saying of the great theologian: 'I haven't the faintest interest in theology which does not help us to evangelize.' Professor Tasker adds: 'And the "theology which helps us to evangelize" is the theology which recognizes "the centrality, the gravity, the inevitableness and the glory of the death of Christ", wherein the unity not only of the New Testament but also of the entire Bible is to be found.'

The Church has done rightly in making much of Good Friday. It is *Good* Friday precisely because it is *God's* Friday (which was the original meaning of the phrase). We cannot meditate too long or too deeply on the great Words from the Cross. Those words have been the source of many a book. Here is another on the same theme.

Mr Val Green believes that the best way to understand the great themes of the Bible is to view them through the eyes of its chief characters. He has led us to the foot of the Cross—that place where was enacted not simply the divine tragedy, but the mighty activity of divine love— and bidden us view it through the eyes of Simon Peter.

We may not agree with all the views expressed by Mr Val Green. But his purpose in writing will have been fulfilled if, as we 'Survey the wondrous Cross where the young Prince of glory died', we meet the eyes of the Master looking into ours. 'The Lord turned and looked on Peter.' May your name and mine take the place of the Apostle as we read this book.

F. D. COGGAN

LONDON COLLEGE OF DIVINITY

ONE

'*The Lord turned and looked upon Peter*'

BEFORE we can approach with fitting reverence and awe this great drama of Good Friday, there are certain scenes at which we must look, in order to get in its true perspective that grim Cross cutting the skyline.

There were those, passing on their way with merchandise, who doubtless in a spirit of curiosity left their caravans and climbed the hill to see why so large a crowd surrounded a cross. But we must not come as curious sightseers. We must realize at the outset that we are to be there as actors in that drama, and so we must get into the atmosphere of our part.

Now, I am going to outline briefly, certain scenes which, though they happened so long ago, have their spiritual parallel in our own lives today. For that purpose I have chosen one character by whose side we will step through these scenes. In fact, we may do more than that, and each of us take the part of Peter in the scenes I am going to sketch. For what one of us has not been in such a case as he on all those steps he took to Calvary?

The character of Peter is so complex that it is typical of normal man. It is a thing of light and shadow, mountain top and valley. In a way it might be called a sane and fair caricature of man's personality. For it is the duty of a caricaturist to emphasize the outstanding qualities of the person caricatured, be they estimable or otherwise, and that is just what Peter's character does to yours and mine. His faults are heavily underlined, his virtues are picked out in letters of gold. So let us trace his companionship with Jesus, and imagine as we do so that we are Peter.

The first association of Peter with Jesus came about in

a natural but very arresting manner. John the Baptist was standing talking to two of his disciples, Andrew and John, when Jesus walked by. Gazing after Him, John spoke as if to himself, these momentous words: 'Behold the Lamb of God.' And the two disciples looked at John the Baptist, realizing the full import of his words, then immediately set out and followed Jesus.

Jesus, sensing their presence, turned round and asked them: 'What seek ye?' And their answer reveals the simple faith they had in John the Baptist's words. They reply: 'Master, where abidest thou?' 'Come and see,' says Jesus, and they accompany Him.

But it is not enough for Andrew that he should have found Jesus himself; his first thought is that he must tell his brother Peter. So, having spent the day with his new-found Master, he sets out to find his brother. What had occurred during that day, what conversation he had had with Jesus, we do not know. But it must have been such as to convince him at the outset of the origin and authority of his Master, for when he comes upon Peter he says to him: 'We have found the Messiah!'

From what we later know of Peter, we can imagine with what impetuous eagerness he accompanied his brother to where Jesus was. And when he came Jesus turned and looked upon him. It was Peter's first experience of those divine eyes, with their deep, understanding look, and that look this time was piercing, kindly, yet considering, as if Jesus were weighing him up and gauging his possibilities.

'Thou art Simon, the son of John,' says Jesus. 'Thou shalt be called Peter.' And Peter means 'rock' or 'stone'. With what omniscience Jesus had plumbed the depths of his character. Below all the uncertainties of his make-up was a stratum of reality, which after the Resurrection was to prove itself virile and effective.

When you first met Jesus, weren't you just like Peter, anxious to please, yet awed and humble? I mean when you were converted. I do not think any of us really met

Him in our early years. In our Sunday-school days He was more or less only a romantic figure of history, not a living personality. But later there came a time when we slowly realized how very present He really is. It was then that He looked upon us with those understanding eyes, and in a moment told us what we really were capable of if we only tried.

The first meeting between Jesus and Peter must not be confused with the call of Peter to discipleship. That was to come later. Jesus had gathered about Him many followers before He chose the twelve who were to be His chosen companions. Our conversion rarely synchronizes with a call to service. First we are prepared as was St Paul in the Street called Straight, by a new knowledge of Jesus as He really is, accompanied by a growing conviction that we can serve Him, and a growing eagerness to start in His service. Then, when we are ready, comes the call.

Peter and Andrew had gone back to their profession—for they were fishermen—just as you and I went about our duties after that first blinding glimpse of the personality of Christ. But he was constantly in their minds. They had seen Him and heard His voice as He spoke to the multitudes.

Then came the call. The day had been very disappointing for the brothers. They had been out fishing, but they had had no success. At last they gave up an apparently hopeless task, and returned to the shore. Leaving their boats well beached, they were busily engaged washing their nets when the sound of a well-known voice caused them to look up. A multitude of men, women and children was slowly approaching the beach, while a Figure which held their attention was walking before, occasionally stopping and turning to teach the people. At last Jesus could go no farther, for He had reached the water's edge. The people were thronging about Him and, looking round, He saw an empty boat which was Peter's, in which He seated

Himself, asking the owner to push a little way out on the water. So Jesus sat in the gently-rocking boat, facing the multitude seated in serried ranks on the ground rising from the lake. 'And he sat down and taught the multitudes out of the boat', St Luke simply puts it.

Having finished His address to the people, Jesus turned and looked upon Peter, a look of confidence and encouragement, and said to him: 'Put out into the deep, and let down your nets for a draught.' And Peter, despite the disappointing day, complied. There must have been something in the look of Jesus that overrode any scruples Peter might have had about a non-fisherman giving him such a command. And his faith in the promise held in that look was fully justified, for he had to call the assistance of the other boats because of the abundance of the fish caught.

Then came the call. So amazed was the fisherman that he fell at Jesus's feet, saying: 'Depart from me; for I am a sinful man, O Lord.' But Jesus answered him: 'Fear not; from henceforth thou shalt catch men.' And Peter forsook all and followed Him.

It was but the step from conversion to service. After that full realization of the reality and virility of the presence of Christ comes that growing realization of His need of us, and our growing eagerness to serve Him. Then, as a kind of shock we discover how utterly unworthy we are to serve Him. That is what Jesus has been waiting for. The period of preparation is over. We are ready for service. It is not until the soul has realized its sin that it is on the way to being saved.

So in the character of Peter we follow Him, accompanied by James and John, leaving behind Zebedee at his mending of the nets. We have looked into the eyes of God and found them very understanding. We have heard His words, 'Come with Me', and have set out on the great adventure of salvation.

The call of Peter as an Apostle came later. Having served his apprenticeship as a disciple or student of Jesus, he was found worthy to be made a leader. There is one interesting point in connexion with the lists of Apostles given in the Gospel history: Peter always heads the list.

I want now to pass on to the next important scene in which Jesus and Peter were the chief characters. Jesus had had a very arduous day, and, having sent away the multitude to whom He had been ministering, He retired to a mountain to pray. The boatmen, of whom Peter was one, who had taken Him across the lake, started to re-cross, but the lakes of Palestine are set at the foot of steep, surrounding hills, through the clefts of which the wind becomes a hurricane and thrashes the water to fury.

A storm sprang up, and that together with the darkness made the position of the rowers one of great peril. It must have been a bad storm to frighten experienced sailors, and we are led to believe that they were in a very nervous state. Suddenly they saw the figure of a man walking toward them on the water. Sailors of all countries are highly superstitious, and these would immediately conclude that it was an apparition. Doubtless they had been thinking and talking about Jesus, for His magnetic personality must have been impossible to forget, and now it would seem to them that they had conjured up some likeness of Him upon the waters, and they would be very fearful.

But Jesus calmed them. 'Be of good cheer,' He said. 'It *is* I; be not afraid.'

And now we have Peter the impetuous again. 'Lord, if it be thou, bid me come unto thee upon the waters,' he called out. Jesus looked upon him and said: 'Come!' What must Peter have read in those divine eyes? There must have been encouragement telling him that he had the power to do this thing, for he swung over the side of the boat and stood up.

But outward circumstances were too strong. He saw the wind-thrashed waves and the shifting waters at his feet. He lost confidence; he began to sink, and in his fear cried out: 'Lord, save me.' So Jesus took his hand

B

and helped him back into the boat saying: 'O thou of little faith, wherefore didst thou doubt?'

How often has that happened to you and me? After our call to service we have tackled some particular job, then it has seemed not so easy as when we first contemplated it, and finally outside circumstances have become too strong for us and we have failed. We would have succeeded had we not been of little faith, and doubted that the power of God through us could accomplish the task.

A small part of the last year of our Lord's ministry had now passed away. During the first two years He had taught and trained His hearers. The last year He reserved to instruct more especially those who were to be His representatives after the Ascension—His Apostles.

There came a time at Capernaum when the disciples of Jesus were faced with two alternatives. They could either accept His sayings, hard though they were, and abide by them no matter what the consequences to themselves, or they could leave Him and again go their own way. And the saying that brought about this crisis is as hard for some today as it was for those early followers: 'Except ye eat the Flesh of the Son of Man and drink His Blood, ye have no life in yourselves.' 'Upon this many of His disciples went back and walked no more with Him.' Then Jesus asked the twelve Apostles: 'Would ye also go away?' Rather than water down His saying, He would sacrifice them too. It was Peter who voiced the opinions of the good companions: 'Lord, to whom shall we go? Thou hast the words of eternal life.' The Lord turned and looked upon Peter then, I believe, and it was a look of love—divine love that bestows largess in a glance. 'Thou art the Holy One of Israel,' concluded Peter. Yes, he was coming to that fullness of understanding which is only arrived at by a companion of God.

And we, too, if we have really striven to understand Jesus, have on occasion felt that inward revelation, that warm glow in our hearts, as if the scarred hand had been placed there in benediction and divine gratitude.

In the world of men in which we live today, there are many opinions about Jesus. There is the Catholic and the Protestant, each with his subdivisions, holding his own view. All these have their own propaganda. There are numerous leaders crying: 'Lo, this is Christ' and 'Lo, this'. Thinking man is torn this way and that by competing ideas and theories concerning the Master. Our world today is no different from that of nineteen hundred years ago.

The Pharisees and the Scribes had their ideas about Him; the poor had theirs. The Greeks and other Gentiles who heard had their conclusions, too. But Jesus alone with His disciples asked them: 'But whom say ye that I am?' Again it is Peter who was the spokesman of the disciples. Probably he was voicing what was only a vague premonition of an idea so far as the rest were concerned, but he wished to be certain in his own mind when he replied: 'Thou art the Christ, the Son of the living God.'

Once again the Lord turned and looked upon Peter, a look of benediction. It takes courage to voice aloud our conviction that Jesus is God, among others who are not yet certain of what He means to them. Have you done it? If you have, then I think you will understand the feeling in Peter's heart when Jesus replied to him: 'Blessed art thou, Simon Bar-jonah, for flesh and blood hath not revealed it unto thee, but My Father which is in heaven.'

But there was a still further reward for the faithful Peter. Jesus said to him: 'Thou art Peter, and upon this rock I will build my Church.' To have confessed Christ before men is to have taken upon yourself the responsibility of being His representative among men. A great responsibility, but how great an honour!

I said at the beginning that Peter's character was a thing of light and shadow, mountain top and valley. He reached the apex of happiness when closest to his Master in thought and deed, as do all of us. At the raising of Jairus's daughter, on the Mount of Transfiguration, in the Garden of Gethsemane, those three occasions when he was one of the chosen three, though he could not fully comprehend all that was happening, Peter was supremely happy, filled, shall we say, with a divine content.

But on his failure to walk on the waters; when Jesus rebuked him as Satan; and in the hall of Caiaphas, he sank into the vale of misery.

Peter's upbringing had been thoroughly orthodox so far as religion went, and he had at the back of his mind all the accretions to the prophetic teaching which were in vogue at that time. Messiah was to come and lead His armies victorious against the Roman oppressor, releasing His oppressed people and reigning from Jerusalem in an eternity of peace and plenty.

When, therefore, Jesus began to prophesy His Passion, judgement, and Crucifixion, Peter was horrified. He had been so taken up with his companionship of Jesus that he had failed to comprehend the full significance of His teaching. It must then have been very mortifying to the Master when Peter rebuked Him for these prophecies, and recalled by his remark anent them the third temptation in the wilderness. But Peter's horror turned to shame when the Lord looked upon him and said: 'Get thee behind Me, Satan; thou art a stumbling block unto Me for thou mindest not the things of God, but the things of men.'

Peter must have known as we know the temptations which Jesus had suffered in the wilderness before His three years' ministry, and to have revived them in his Master's mind by his own carelessness must have caused him sorrow. The look of our Lord on this occasion must have held some of the horror and loathing which the memory of the temptations brought back. And if we strive in any way but the way of Jesus to bring about God's will we are calling up those early sufferings of Christ, and clothing ourselves in His sight with all their loathsomeness and hypocrisy.

Peter was still further to cause his Master sorrow. Jesus strove to point out to him his wickedness in the incident just narrated. It may have been a harsh way of doing it, but Peter's self-confidence was such that it must be broken down ruthlessly if it was to be destroyed utterly.

Just before the Gethsemane scene Jesus again issued a warning. 'Though all may be offended in Thee,' boasts Peter, 'yet will not I be offended.' Jesus looked upon him, a look of compassion for his weakness, and said to him: 'Verily I say unto thee, that this night, before the cock crow, thou shalt deny Me thrice.' But even this rebuke with its foreboding, did not shake the self-confidence of Peter. 'Even if I must die with Thee, yet will I not deny Thee.'

Now let us go into the hall of Caiaphas. It was crowded with a motley throng. There were the Scribes and Pharisees, bitter in their hatred of Jesus, and the many whom they had bribed or bullied into being hostile to anything but the death sentence. There were also many who had followed Jesus, or been helped by Him in some moral or physical way. And, dignified and aloof there were the Roman guards and court officials. To them all Jews were rabble and beneath contempt.

Into this throng came Peter, brought by the quiet and faithful John. Peter's chief weakness was a fear of physical injury. It is a failing in which most of mankind can sympathize with him. This fear would, under ordinary circumstances, have kept him away from the field of danger. But there was a counterbalancing love for his Master. Torn between the two, Peter summoned up enough courage to go to the trial of Jesus. John, it would appear, passed on into the audience chamber, Peter was left behind in the court.

I may be wrong, but I feel that, lacking the companionship of John on the way to the trial, Peter would never have got as far as the court. Now, however, that companionship was taken away, and he was alone in an alien atmosphere.

What conflicting thoughts struggled for control of his mind? His early teaching asserted itself. When the Messiah came, was He not going to sweep all before Him? What power could the Roman Empire possibly have against the Chosen of God? Yet, there on the dais stood Jesus, bound with a thong, helpless. Nor did He seem even to be bothering to defend Himself against all the false accusations. Could this then be the Messiah? Against this insidious undermining thought came another arrayed in the friendship which he really had in his heart for the Master. Following this came the memory of those scenes when Jesus had displayed His power over disease and death and the devils themselves. It might be that a miracle was going to happen, as it had so often happened during his year with Jesus.

The cold assailed Peter, but was it physical cold or the result of fear? He went to the fire in the middle of the hall and started to warm his hands. In the firelight his eyes were filled with uncertainty and fear alternately; his hands trembled. A certain maid, seeing him as he sat in the light of the fire, said: 'This man also was with Him.' Fear sprang into the eyes of Peter—stark, staring fear of physical hurt. 'I know Him not.' The words were out before he realized that he had spoken.

It was not over yet; a little while later a man looked at him and said: 'Thou also art one of them.' Would they never leave him alone? He glared round at his accuser. 'Man, I am not,' he shouted.

So, for the space of an hour he was tortured by accusing looks and glances of suspicion, till at last a man approached him, and, drawing the attention of the others about him, said: 'Of a truth this man also was with Him, for he is a Galilean.' Peter was desperate. Jesus had still shown no sign of trying to extricate Himself from His terrible position. Perhaps after all He was only a fake. There had been others before.

You and I are Peter in this great crisis of his life. There have been moments in our lives when we have wondered why certain things were allowed to happen if God is a God of love. And maybe there have been moments in the lives of some when sticking to the side of Jesus has meant scoffing and perhaps suffering as a reward. If in those moments of trial they have failed, then they know what made Peter cry out in an agony of fear: 'Man, I know not what thou sayest.'

'And, immediately, while he yet spake, the cock crew.'

I can imagine that denial of Peter's tailing off falteringly as the crowing of the cock recalled the prophecy of his Master. It recalled so much that prophecy, all the spiritual side of the Master's teaching. He had never claimed, he had always denied, an earthly kingdom.

Tremblingly Peter turned toward the dais. 'And the Lord turned, and looked upon Peter.' How he had hurt Jesus, Peter could see reflected in that look. It was not a look of accusation, but one of love, and of pity for the Apostle's weakness and lack of understanding. And Peter went out, weeping bitterly.

Nothing is more terribly heartrending than to see a strong man weep. Yet those tears were the outward and visible sign of the purifying of Peter's character. Again he had descended into the vale of misery. He was one of those of whom the Psalmist's words might be used: 'Who, going through the vale of misery, use it for a well.' His tears were the cleansing waters of his soul, and out of this grim experience he was able to draw new strength and resolution.

This brief sketch of Peter's character will, I hope, help us, through his eyes, to see more clearly the full significance for us of Calvary. For the progress of Peter's soul from conversion to companionship is that of the normal Christian.

Too often people are churchgoers, nominal Christians, because they have been brought up in that way. And there are those who live and die without the knowledge or experience of conversion. They live naturally good lives, or fulfil the principle of Christ's teaching because they realize it is their duty to society to do so, but to neither of these two classes is the pleasure of sharing with Christ in the scheme of salvation ever revealed.

To many, however, comes a time when there is a glimmer of some hidden meaning and glory in this Christianity they have embraced nominally for so long. They have, if they could realize it, met Jesus for the first time. And that is the first of a series of incidents and circumstances which draw them nearer and nearer to Christ until they are in truth followers of Him. But it is not until they have realized their own unworthiness and unreliability, and discovered that they must have Jesus within them on whom to rely, that companionship of Jesus with all its mystic meaning and its compensating happiness for worldly pleasures denied, is vouchsafed to them.

Such was Peter's case, and you and I are mirrors of Peter. To some have come that apex of happiness—companionship of Jesus. Others may still just be followers. And there may be some who have not yet met Him in His startling, vital understanding of modern human difficulties. No matter to what stage of the soul's progress we have arrived, let us all, through the eyes of Peter, watch the greatest drama of the ages.

TWO

'Father, forgive them; for they know not what they do'

ARRIVING at the court-house of Pilate's judgement hall, Peter wandered aimlessly up and down. Shame and contrition for his cowardly betrayal of his Master blinded him to what was going on around him. The confused babble of voices from the building came to him, modulated by the sultry air. From the judgement hall itself an ever-increasing clamour reached his ears.

'Crucify Him!' 'Barabbas!' 'Thou art not Caesar's friend!' 'Give us Barabbas!' Accusations and insults rose like frenzied shrieks above the howling of the mob. Peter stood, listened intently even, I believe, and went to the door of the judgement hall. Anger rose up within him; his impetuous nature would even then, if the memory of his betrayal had not been so recent and so bitter, have brought him into physical conflict with the detractors of Jesus.

He stood at the door and listened. The clamour died down; for a space there was dead silence, except for the suggestion of one voice speaking, though he could not catch the words. Then came again the frenzied clamour, and the words were now more or less distinct: 'His blood be upon us and on our children.'

Followed the sound of many feet, and the court emptied. Still Peter stood, his mind confused, and striving to get things clear. Leaning against the wall, taking no notice of the damsel who looked at him and then pointed him out to her companions as they left the court-house, he was lost in miserable speculation.

Of a definitely militant nature, he had expected that this was He who should redeem Israel; but the method used by Jesus was not the method Peter either expected or approved. Peter, before his conversion, preferred the title 'Prince of Israel' to 'Messiah' for Jesus. His conception of the Messianic prophecies was a thoroughly militaristic one, as was that of the bulk of the Jewish race. Yet, outside Gethsemane, Jesus had said, 'Put up your sword,' and had healed the first and only wound of the battle. That attitude on that occasion had been a distinct shock to Peter. With the rest of the disciples, he had forsaken Christ and fled.

Could this man, so different from anything that anyone had expected, really be the Saviour of Israel? That was the question which baffled the reasoning powers of Peter. The rabbis had so consistently taught that His kingdom when He came was to be of this world, that it is small wonder that His arrest and death were a shock to His followers.

Peter and his nation had made the mistake which is made in our own time over and over again by followers of Jesus. He had striven to fit Jesus into his own preconceived notions of what Jesus should be like, instead of fitting himself and his ideas to the Jesus whom he knew.

'My kingdom is not of this world.' The sentence leapt into Peter's mind. Jesus had said that, of course, and it had puzzled His disciples quite a lot. They had talked about it among themselves afterwards, but had been unable to arrive at any clear understanding of its meaning. Now it started another train of thought in the mind of Peter. But that thought was interrupted.

Coming from a distance was the noise of brutal laughter. It was behind the wall, in the courtyard of the judgement hall. Odd scraps of words came to his ears. 'Prophesy— who struck Thee?' 'Hail, King!' Not satisfied with accomplishing His conviction, the soldiers were torturing and taunting Him. It was more than Peter could stand, and he hurried away. If only he could find the other disciples, they might be able to accomplish His rescue.

He searched everywhere among the jostling crowds waiting for the procession to Calvary to commence, but nowhere could he find any of his friends. Many gazed at him suspiciously as a known follower of the Galilean, and wondered at the purposefulness in his eyes and bearing. In his brusque way he brushed past and through the surging masses of people, oblivious of the motions, words, and glances thrown at him as he went.

At last he realized the futility of striving to find his friends among the gathering thousands, and a wave of excitement passing along the crowd drew his attention. Nearer and nearer came the roar, and at last he was able to distinguish the words: 'He comes!' People began to jump upon each other's shoulders, hoping to see the distant, approaching Figure. Men, with coarse jests, held wives and sweethearts above their heads, and asked for information of what was happening to be passed down to them.

The bull-like figure of Peter grew restive against inaction. He could hardly move his arms; the press was so great. The smell of hot, crowded humanity was obnoxious. But, above all, he must know what was going forward. Cleaving with his arms, as a swimmer against an angry sea, he pressed slowly nearer and nearer to the narrow channel through the sea of faces, kept clear by the Roman soldiers. At last he stood in the front rank bordering the open path along which in the distance his Master was toiling toward him beneath the heavy Cross.

His eyes ached, so intense was his gaze on the approaching Figure. His progress was slow, not so much at first because of the heavy burden of the Cross, but on account of the numerous men and women, some with young children, who sought His aid from their physical ailments on this His last itinerary.

The power of Jesus had always fascinated Peter. He had seen the devils themselves subject to his Master, and the fury of the waves abate at His word. What now puzzled the Apostle was that, with such power, He should

be content to waste it in healing sickness when He might
have turned its full force against His accusers and His
guards, and thereby won freedom for Himself. Peter,
who himself had little self-control, could not understand or
appreciate it in others. The type of person of whom
Peter was representative before his conversion looks upon
self-control as a sign of weakness, instead of an exhibition
of strength, and refers to its possessors as 'soft'.

The hand of Jesus was never still on that last journey,
nor His eyes bent down. The weak were made strong,
their physical defects removed, and many who, but a
short time before, had cried, 'His blood be upon us and
on our children!' began to cease their clamour and blasphemy against Him as they saw no sign of dejection in
His spirit, but rather the slow, triumphal march of a
victor.

Even when He fell through physical fatigue beneath
the weight of the Cross, their jeering laughter was cut
short at the uncomplaining steadfastness of His eyes as
He rose to His feet again. Again He stumbled, and it
was with greater difficulty that, under the Roman lash,
He was able to get up again.

There was a commotion in the crowd, and a tall, burly
man was seen pushing his way through the people,
which parted like straws before his flaying arms. Jesus
was striving to rise, and a Roman soldier, seeing this
young giant gazing on in speechless anger at the cruelty
Jesus was suffering, seized this young man, Simon of
Cyrene, and dragging him forward compelled him to take
up the Cross of Jesus.

I wonder—did Simon need compelling? But what of
Peter? I can see the blush of shame rushing over his face.
Simon was no bigger than he—and Simon was a complete
stranger compared with Peter's association with Jesus.
Why, then, had *he* not gone and taken the Cross of his
Master and *offered* to carry it? Is it an omen? Has he,
whom his Master said was to be the chief of the Apostles,
been superceded because of his act of treachery? All

these questions gnawed at the *distrait* mind of the watching Apostle.

This incident was the first of many which were to occur during the grim tragedy of Calvary, all of which were to have the effect of driving farther and deeper home the shame and humiliation which was to bring about the true and full conversion of Peter.

The surging crowd on either side strove to keep pace with Jesus; some scoffing, some praising, others pleading for help. But none strove harder than Peter to keep beside his Lord. Yet the Cross was between them, and hindered the Apostle from catching the Master's eye.

The Cross—which from now on was to be symbolic of the faith, with all its difficulties and consequent sacrifices—had cast its shadow between Peter and Jesus on more than one occasion. Now its reality proved a true barrier to that interchange of confidence which was essential to true Apostleship.

So the procession moved forward, like some great organ music, its harmonies hidden away, occasionally revealing themselves, but more often drowned by the deep diapason of the Jewish wrath against the Messiah. With it went Peter, his mind now numbed by a great fear—fear of separation from Jesus, of whom his heart had become an integral part. Had he followed the dictates of his heart in the first place, all would have been well, but he appealed to reason, and reason is finite, and incapable of comprehending the infinite.

Forward, with dragging steps, went Jesus, weak through loss of blood drawn by the thongs with which they thrashed Him e'er He set out. His eyes were steadfast and merciful, containing no hint of weariness or hostility. 'Like a lamb before its shearers is dumb, so opened He not His mouth.' His manhood was as our manhood, there was nothing superhuman about it; He had emptied Himself of His Godhead before He took upon Him mortal flesh, and so as He grew more and more feeble the procession moved with slower pace. The heat of the day grew oppressive, and the crowd slowly became silent through exhaustion, until—on the summit of that tragic hill—a silence somewhat ominous fell upon that vast assemblage.

Only the brutal laughter and coarse jests of the Roman soldiers, modulated by the sultry air, broke that awful stillness. Upon the cross, now lying on the ground, they placed His tired body. On the fastening of Him to that Cross I will not dwell. It was too horrible a procedure, and it too nearly concerns us each individually, for us to be able to bear to stand and watch.

Peter stood for a moment, craning over the heads of others to see what was happening, then, with a wrenching sob, he flung away from the crowd.

Surely this was the end, he thought. Up to the very last moment he had been hoping for one of those amazing miracles which would have awed the crowd to its knees, and delivered his Master free and victorious to His disciples again. But now, pinned down to that rude Cross, what chance had He of delivering Himself? 'None!' said Peter audibly as he rushed away.

But the bond between himself and Jesus was too strong for him to go far. A thought struck him. When the Cross was lifted up and set in its socket, Jesus would be high above the heads of the crowd. Maybe his Master would look upon him and forgive him for his weakness and his treachery. He stopped his headlong flight. I feel that Peter would have gone through fire to receive that look of forgiveness from Jesus. Slowly he turned back and threaded his way through the people.

It was not so difficult for Peter to get back as he had thought it would be. The crowd was thinning. Many of those who loved Jesus, and had benefited by His healing power or His sympathetic understanding, were hurrying, weeping, to Jerusalem. Many Peter recognized: a man who was lame, a boy who had been possessed by a devil, a cleansed leper; all with that same set expression— heart-rending anguish, blended with a hatred of His enemies, whom they thrust out of their way as they went.

The sight of these poor people looking so lost increased the anguish in Peter's heart. He remembered a time when his wife's mother was lying critically ill at home, and Jesus had come and touched her, and the fever had left her immediately. His was a grief too strong for tears, but the constriction at his throat became an agony.

At last he arrived at the front of the crowd watching the Crucifixion from a little distance down the hill. They were all too intent on drinking in the details of the terrible scene before them to notice him. Jesus, His limbs taut upon the Cross, gazed down in His agony upon the up-turned faces. At His feet the Roman soldiers were dicing for His seamless robe, and their callous indifference to what was happening above their heads, together with their coarse talk, typified the Roman brutality of the time. Peter's face was among those upturned to Jesus, but his wore no expression of malevolent triumph, as did some of the others. His face was white, like drawn parchment, trans-parent-looking against the black of his beard; and his eyes, hot and aching, were endeavouring to catch those of the Saviour. Yet, though the glance of Jesus passed over the faces below Him, His eyes never seemed to focus on Peter's.

As he gazed upward, and saw his Master's Cross reach-ing up into the sky, a phrase once used by Jesus flashed back into his mind: 'I, if I be lifted up,' Jesus had said, 'will draw all men unto Me.' 'Lifted up'! Peter's eyes sought the ground while the application of the phrase to present circumstances dawned upon him. Here, on this hill which climbed up above the Holy City, hanging still higher on the lofty Cross, was He who had spoken those words. Could this be what He had meant? Were His words a prophecy? And if so, what did they mean?

Peter was conscious of Jerusalem at the foot of the hill behind him, and of the towering figure before him at the top, and the association of the two brought back into his mind another incident. Jesus had once told him of the happenings during those forty days spent in the wilderness while He was tempted. One of those incidents now stood starkly out in Peter's mind. The devil had taken his Master to the top of a high hill, and from its summit shown Him a panorama of the whole world, promising Him this in return for devil-worship. Jesus had brusquely refused.

And now the scene appeared to be repeated in a different form. High and lifted up, He surveyed the panorama containing the Holy City as its point of concentration. The devil had promised Him on the former occasion the kingdoms of the world and the glory of them, and He had refused. Now a new interpretation of His teaching suggested itself to Peter. Thus, lifted up, He was to draw all men unto Him. For their kingdom He cared nothing, it was the men themselves He wanted.

This was the nearest approach to complete revelation that Peter received. He paralleled the two scenes in his mind, and strove to see their connexion. The devil was the representative of worldly powers; that much was certain. Had Jesus then fallen in with the devil's offer, would He not have been just the type of Messiah the rabbis had taught them to expect? At the thought Peter started. Was that the reason for Jesus's many outbursts against the Scribes and Pharisees as fools and hypocrites, blind leading the blind? And before Him, John the Baptist had called them a generation of vipers and warned them of wrath to come. Surely this must be the true lesson of that withstood temptation.

On the other hand, there was the grim scene being enacted before him. Again he was on a hill overlooking the earth. Again this time it was the devil, representative of the wickedness and vileness of men, who had put him there, and the thought compelled itself into the mind of Peter, that they had been led by the Scribes and Pharisees. Over against this was the prophecy of Jesus that, being thus lifted up, He would draw all men unto Him. Surely he—Peter—had been guilty of expecting the devil's way of conquest—kingdoms falling before a militarist Messiah; power and glory of an earthly kind accruing to the victor.

This logical reasoning was not impossible to the Peter who was so logically on that first Pentecostal morning so concisely to prove from Scripture the validity of the claims of Jesus.

This problem of that day has its modern counterpart. Why does not the Church force the heads of governments, when anti-Christian laws are promulgated, to abandon their project? asks the modern man. And here is his answer, straight from the Cross. Christianity is a religion of love, a compelling love which knows nothing of force, for it compels by attraction, and a love which works for the salvation of individual souls, not the mass salvation of a nation.

The glory of the revelation which had come to Peter did much to alleviate his grief; yet that revelation contained a sting. He himself had been one of those whose views were the views of the devil in that early temptation of Jesus. He looked up again to the face of Jesus; but still, no matter how he tried, he could not catch the eye of the Master. Sorrow claimed him again. Was the sin of his denial past all forgiveness? Did all the months of companionship with the Messiah count for nothing? Were the glorious moments when he won Christ's approbation lost in the mists of forgotten things?

Now, though Peter had got so far as to see that Christ's way was the right way, in his cogitations the Cross was still a stumbling-block to his complete understanding. Jesus lifted up was to draw all men unto Him—but how? There was a finality about death in the pre-Resurrection mind of Peter, which built up all sorts of obstacles to the fruition of this prophecy. This problem was to haunt him, unsolved until the morning of the Resurrection.

Tired with grief and much thought, he gazed with puzzled awe at the Cross before him, a strange expectation

c

in his heart that yet something might happen which would clear up his remaining difficulty.

While he is thus gazing, let us not forget that we are striving to put ourselves in the place of Peter. His problems, his questions, are the problems and questions of mankind today. Not only do some men in our time ask why the Church—which is the Body of Christ on earth—does not assert itself in international matters, but they also ask questions concerning Christ Himself which betray a mind as mobile and unstable as was Peter's at the Crucifixion. They cannot understand the Christian interpretation of the word 'love'. They are as yet unable to realize that to the said Christian love is a quiet penetration of the individual soul by the personality of Jesus, not an army with banners treading underfoot the souls which do not accept it. That is why, from a religious point of view, the Crusades were such unfortunate incidents in the history of Christianity. Once force allies itself to love, love retreats and leaves force to work out its relentless course.

A modern application of this principle is found in the tackling of the problem of the slums. Authority, taking the matter in hand with all the machinery of officialdom at its disposal, has created discord and sordid discussion. Landlords have objected strongly to the forcing of their hands in the matter, and complained bitterly at the financial loss in which it has involved them. Yet there are hundreds of landlords who have been penetrated by the personality of Christ, and have voluntarily reconditioned their property, even going so far as to pull down the old and construct liveable habitations, at great financial loss to themselves. The Church has thus in its own quiet fashion—which is the fashion of love—through individuals, tackled this large problem.

As in the larger, so in the smaller, individual modern questions, this principle works out. The person who feels that he is compelled by authority to bring himself into accord with the rules of good-citizenship often rebels, and crime is the consequence; but the individual who has learnt fellowship and love from the example of Christ is an ideal citizen, voluntarily.

But to return to Peter: we have seen how far his reasoning had led him; let us again company with him and follow the working of his mind.

It was with difficulty that he thought clearly because of the personal anguish caused by the suffering of Jesus before him. Granted that this was the Messiah, the long-promised Saviour of Israel; and granted also that it was the souls of men more than their bodies, their God-nearness rather than their worldly wealth or power, which concerned Him most, and for which He strove, how was His death going to help them? As I have already said, in the mind of Peter at that time there was a finality about death that brooded no speculation as to the future. If this was the way in which Christ was to win the kingdoms of the souls of men, how was it going to happen, seeing He had but a few short hours to live, and those hours were to be spent in suffering?

We will see, as we follow Peter through the drama of Calvary, the slow dawning of a possible meaning of the Cross, a meaning which was to be confirmed by Jesus Himself at a later date. At present, the more he thought about the problem, the more confused he became. The drawn-out agonizing of the Master he loved so dearly, and his disloyalty to whom was a constant stab at his heart, numbed all his faculties, until he was incapable of reasoning as he would.

It seemed that hours had passed since he returned from his headlong flight to see Jesus high and lifted up on the Cross, yet time had measured it only by a few minutes. Unlike the thieves crucified on either side of Him, who struggled in their bonds, cursing their persecutors, Jesus hung quiet, His eyes only moving, looking into the faces below Him or turned upwards in silent prayer.

This stillness in Jesus had always puzzled Peter. He himself was a blustering fellow, always on the move, whose dynamic personality found expression only in action. The time when Jesus had flogged the money-changers out of the Temple had been a moment after Peter's own heart, but it was an isolated incident. On the whole he could never remember meeting anyone so quiet as Jesus. When the disciples had returned from that first missionary journey, Peter had been ready to burst forth with a glowing account of all that they had done, but Jesus had quietly said: 'Come ye yourselves apart and rest awhile.' And those hours which the Master had spent alone on the mountain-side in prayer had puzzled the Apostle greatly. He himself liked plenty of company and action. Yet he had to confess that rest after the missionary journey had given him time to think, and many events which had happened during that time, and which he had forgotten, came back into his mind vividly and with new meaning. Also he could not deny that, after His quiet time following an arduous day, Jesus was just as magnetic as in the early dawn.

Yet this stillness of Jesus on the Cross was different: it had an air of finality about it that could not be associated with the quiet times during the ministry. In His very glance there was an air of submission, but Peter was to learn that it was not submission to the ruthless will of men, but obedience to the Will of God.

Silence is always rather terrifying to those who have not learnt its value. The clank and clamour of the mechanical age in which we live gives us little opportunity for being quiet. But there is time and opportunity for this restorative of the soul for those who care enough to find it. Your town-dweller who is immersed in the round of work and pleasure which the town affords cannot stand a holiday in the country. They have had all their thinking done for them by stage and screen, and the silence (which they do not know how to occupy) of the woods and fells appals them. Yet the wear and tear of the workaday world on the human soul, which never uses the restorative of silence, brings spiritual death which we see so often in the eyes of the young today. Children of the machine, they might be called, automatons, getting up, going to work, eating, going to pleasure, going to bed, with everything bar their eating and sleeping done for them by the mechanized age wherein we live—while one hour of silence and quiet reflection each day would keep alight within them the Divine spark, and restore the sense of values they have lost.

The art of being still is all the more necessary to the person who is naturally of an active disposition, as Peter himself was to learn; it is the art of submitting one's will to God.

The crowd about the Cross, gaining confidence again by the apparent submission of their Victim, was by no means silent. Coarse jests were flung at Jesus, and His character and work talked about and discussed loudly, while the word 'impostor' was frequently heard. The Scribes and Pharisees, gazing on their handiwork, were obviously well satisfied with the way things had turned out. They were avenged on Him who had called them fools and hypocrites. The armour which He had pierced so deeply by His ruthless criticism was again restored to its impregnability by their self-conceit.

Peter felt a wrath against them which suddenly turned upon himself. Was he not in like case? Had he not believed in the type of Messiah they expected? And when disappointed had he not sided by his very treachery with them? Self-contempt overwhelmed him. He who had always been so proud of his strength of character, and so sure of himself, was on a level with fools and hypocrites.

It was at this moment that Jesus spoke those first words from the Cross: 'Father, forgive them, for they know not what they do.' And they fell upon the startled ears of Peter like a benediction. 'Forgive'! His heart had been silently crying out that word in supplication ever after Jesus had turned and looked upon him, and now his eyes in anxious hope sought again those of the Master. But still he was unable to obtain a glance from Jesus.

What had He said? '*Father*, forgive them.' He who had said to the sick of the palsy and to countless others, 'Thy sins be forgiven thee', was pleading to His Father to forgive them this greatest sin. Was forgiveness for it so uncertain? Was the Master Himself not prepared to grant it, that He referred it to a Higher Authority? Yet was there not hope in the phrase itself? If Jesus so strongly desired their forgiveness was not that desire promoted from out a forgiving heart? Peter felt hope anew springing up within him. The problem of the death of the Messiah had precluded as yet any speculation as to the future, but the love he bore his Master, and the sorrow he had for his own disloyalty, made forgiveness now, before He died, essential to the penitent Peter.

The Apostle had no hesitation in placing himself in the category of those needing forgiveness, and seeing in the supplication of Jesus a petition on his own behalf. He had not yet received the fullness of vision wherein he would ultimately perceive that the sins of all humanity in all time were included in that Divine prayer. Had he seen that now, the full significance of Calvary would have flashed upon his consciousness. He was to suffer more pangs of regret for his sin before that complete scheme of salvation which contained the Cross was made manifest to him.

The Crucifixion of Jesus, which took place in time, must be viewed from the standpoint of eternity. We must think of it as taking place now and always, the sins of present and all mankind, through their folly and hypocrisy, nailing Him to the Cross. Then His words will reveal their full significance. 'Father, forgive them, for they know not what they do' applies to you and to me. Here we can see how representative Peter is of present-day mankind in all its misunderstanding of Christ, or its indifference to Him, or its betrayal of Him by its words or its deeds, or its forsaking of Him because His sayings are too hard for it. That cry of our Lord rings down the ages into *our* ears, and sinfully stupid we would be if there were no repentant response to it in our hearts.

The effect upon the crowd interested Peter as it should interest us in retrospect. That crowd was made up of normal men and women of the age, an age no different in its human components from our own or any age. Some were struck silent as its meaning thrust through their outer complacency and stirred, however faintly, an answering chord; some laughed hysterically because they were afraid that if they showed any response to it they would be laughed at by their friends; some increased their blasphemy out of sheer bravado, not daring to admit a greater personality than their own. On the ears of others it had no effect whatever, and they continued their conversations uninterrupted. All these types are in our midst today.

All that went on around Peter was seen by him as in a dream. Later it was all to come back to him in startling vividness, but for the moment it only impinged upon his subconscious mind, so concentrated was his attention upon his Master, and on the implication for him of the words spoken by the dying Christ. Jesus had so often mentioned the forgiveness of sins, and so often had cleansed those who came to Him of their sins first and their physical infirmities later. This was the characteristic in the method and teaching of Jesus which had appeared so diametrically opposed to the rabbinical picture of the coming Messiah. 'Forgive your enemies, do good to those that persecute you.' 'Turn the other cheek.' These had been hard sayings to the Jews with their pride of race, when thought of in conjunction with their Roman oppressors. And it was these oppressors from whom they had expected Messiah to free them. To Peter, the wordly impetuous, this forgiveness of enemies and turning the other cheek had been hard sayings indeed. Yet when he was in the position of the enemy, as now—for had he not sworn that he knew not Jesus?—how he craved for that forgiveness, and how he longed that Jesus would look with forgiving eyes upon him.

Thus he stood, gazing at Jesus, oblivious of all that went on around him, an earnest expectation in his heart. But it was not yet to be. His soul was to sink to even deeper depths of misery and penitence before Jesus considered that the time had come to reinstate him in His favour.

THREE

'Today shalt thou be with Me in Paradise'

IF THE agonized plea on their behalf, 'Father, forgive
them, for they know not what they do', had stunned
some of the contemporaries of Jesus to wondering silence,
it had increased the ribaldry of others. Their laughter
became more brutal, their revilings more coarse. Had
they not fastened Him well! Nailed as He was to the
Cross what fear need they have of that miraculous power
which He had so often displayed before their eyes?
Gradually their language and blasphemous merriment
broke through the mental isolation of Peter, and he
burned with anger at them and shame at his own im-
potence to stop them. He heard the Scribes and Pharisees,
who had feared Him and not dared ever to contradict
Him when He was free, scoffing and jeering at Him.
'He saved others,' one shouted to the crowd, 'let Him
save Himself, if this is the Christ of God, His Chosen.'
Then another shouted with coarse laughter: 'Let Him
now come down from the Cross and we will believe on
Him.'

That last phrase stabbed right through Peter's mind
recalling his former thoughts. 'Let Him come down': of
what did those words remind him? Before Jesus had
spoken those words of prayer for their forgiveness, Peter's
mind had been dwelling on the Forty Days of the Temptation as recounted to His Apostles by Jesus, and particularly
had he been impressed by the connexion between the
devil's offer of the whole world after he had lifted the
Master to the top of a mountain and shown it to Him, in
return for devil-worship. Now another link was formed
between the Temptation and Calvary. Had not Jesus
told how the devil had placed Him upon a pinnacle of

the Temple, and tempted Him to cast Himself down in order to prove to the passing throng below that He was God's Son? Peter remembered poignantly the eyes of Jesus as He recalled that temptation. They had blazed with anger at the effrontery of the devil and at his misquotation of Scripture in support of his plea.

Here before the Apostle the scene was being repeated as the scene of Jesus high and lifted up upon the mountain was also being repeated. Men were taking upon their lips the tempting words of the devil: 'Let Him now come down and we will believe on Him.' Again it was pressed home to Peter that in this terrible drama before him men were taking the devil's part. Again the complement of that thought thrust itself into his mind, if the destruction of Jesus was the work of the devil by man's agency, then Jesus must be of God.

It was now I imagine that the sacrificial conception of Calvary began to dawn upon the penitent Peter. He cast his mind back to the beginning of this drama to the time he had spent in the council chamber, looking toward the central Figure of that terrible scene. Jesus, quietly, had stood facing a timid Judge and a bought jury. The scene had not been one of tenseness as we know it during the hearing of a big case in our own courts. There was confusion of tongues, and voice lifted against voice. There was revealed in voice and gesture the blood-lust. Yet in the midst of it all, knowing full well the outcome, seeing in His mind's eye the Cross already limned against the skyline, Jesus had stood calm and unmoved. Many artists have painted that picture, but none, I believe, has got that look of introspection in the eyes of the Saviour which I am sure was there.

Jesus had not even answered the accusing Scribes and Pharisees. His replies to Pilate himself had been brief and, to the Governor, unintelligible but strongly perturbing. It had seemed as if Jesus was forcing His mind in upon Himself and only vaguely was aware of the scene around Him.

It had been a strange trial, one that would be called sensational in the full sense of the word by a Court reporter of our day. There had been constant interruptions and disorderly scenes. The least moved Figure in the packed Court during the whole proceedings had been the Accused Himself.

Peter's denial of the Master had come before the trial had progressed far, and his breath still hurt him as he thought of that ignominious moment. Yet though his own cowardice had driven him forth from the council chamber his mind had stayed behind with Jesus. I imagine that for a moment Peter had thought of himself as a second Judas. But there had been a big difference between their methods of betrayal, as Peter himself was to discover upon reflection. Judas had sold the Master for thirty pieces of silver to the enemy, but what had Peter gained by denying knowledge of Jesus? There had been no thought in his mind of personal gain. His crime had not been premeditated as was that of Judas Iscariot. It had been the weakness of a moment, for which at his own crucifixion later he was voluntarily to pay the price.

The trial had dragged its way on while Peter had stood outside, his thoughts upon his own weakness growing more and more bitter as the time wore on. At last the trial had ended. Satisfied with the turn of events and clapped on the back by the Scribes and Pharisees, who flattered them for their just decision regarding the fate of Jesus, the rabble had begun to pour out of the judgement hall. With ribaldry and coarse jest they had filed through the doorways, passing the penitent Peter as he had stood disconsolate by the wall.

The sight of the mob moving past him had brought him out of his reverie. From the occasional remarks from the passing crowd he had gathered what decision had been given. Then Jesus, his Master, was to be crucified. This had indeed appeared to be the end of all his hopes. He had thought that this was He that should redeem Israel, but at that moment his beliefs had lain in ruins about him. Death! The thought had forced itself upon him: crucifixion meant death, and beyond death what appeal was there?

In his helpless and disconsolate rage he had looked upon the moving people who had hounded Pilate to this decision, and to his mind in its then state they had appeared no more than a crowd of jackals who, having worked their will upon their victim, leave him for further conquests. Animals! Yes, that was what they were, he had decided, animals without reason, who could be made to obey a stronger will for a few paltry shekels just as a dog did the will of its master for a basin of food. Like animals, too, they were happy when flattered and patted on the back for performing their duty satisfactorily; snarling and dangerous if any opposed the will of their masters. Then the same thought had turned upon himself. We are too prone to fit criticisms to the backs of others to notice what well-fitting garments they make for ourselves. Peter had realized that what had passed through his mind concerning those before him applied equally well within. He himself had not shouted 'Crucify Him', nor had he demanded the blood of Jesus, yet in his own way he had sunk as low. Because we do not openly vilify Christ does not qualify us for condemning openly those who do. It behoves us to look within us to see if we do not sometimes by our very silences when He is traduced, sin as greatly as they. This Peter had realized, and, realizing, was covered with shame.

Peter looked out now upon the same crowd, and a thought which before had been interrupted by his desire to find the other Apostles came back into his mind. Stray words and phrases of Jesus had prompted this thought. It was a strange thought, a thought that was to recur time and again during the drama of Calvary. The picture of Christ on the dais in the council chamber of Caiaphas continued throughout this thought-process at the back of his mind, like the scenery on a stage. And it was this picture itself which in the first place had suggested the germ of the idea he was now trying to develop, and which now occupied him. How silent and submissive Jesus had been, this thought ran, and called up another picture out of the writings of the prophet Isaiah: 'Like a lamb before his shearers is dumb so opened he not his mouth.'

The phrase so aptly portrayed the attitude of Jesus during His trial that Peter pondered it. The prophecy of Isaiah would be as familiar as other Old Testament writings to him, but this saying had never before occurred to him in connexion with the Messiah. If Jesus was the long-expected Saviour and this phrase so vividly described His reaction to His traducers, then surely his, Peter's, conception, and the conception of the whole of orthodox Judaism concerning the Messiah was very far wrong.

Could this refer to the Messiah? Was it possible for anyone to conquer by submission? Was the orthodox military conception of Messiah nearer to what one could logically expect? To the robust Peter force was more significant than acquiescence. Yet his thoughts having once begun to wander away among the prophets an incident came to his mind to support the idea of a lamb-like Christ. Had not Elijah spoken with God? How was it that the account ran? 'Behold the Lord passed by, and a great and strong wind rent the mountains, and brake in pieces the rocks before the Lord; but the Lord was not in the wind: and after the wind an earthquake; but the Lord was not in the earthquake: and after the earthquake a fire; but the Lord was not in the fire: and after the fire a still, small voice.' That fitted exactly.

To us two thousand years later the evolution of man's idea of God is already clearly defined by a study of the biblical writings in their chronological order. We can see at a glance how man came to look upon God as a superman, and attributed to Him the characteristics he most admired in his fellow men, the chief of these being power and strength. To Peter in those infant years of theology such reasoning was impossible, but this picture of Elijah discovering God to be not force, but calmness, so fitted as did Isaiah's symbol of the lamb, the Master's attitude, that it set his mind in a whirl of conjecture. So it was to remain, with occasional gleams of revelation lighting the darkness of his mind, and slowly discovering for him the reason for and meaning of the Crucifixion of Jesus, all through the drama of Calvary.

Calvary must ever be looked upon as an act of submission that has impressed the whole world more than all the armies with banners, and the great onslaughts of military leaders; an act more heroic than any before or since in the annals of mankind. It comes as a shock to the worldly person whose sole ambition is self-aggrandisement, to realize that there is any courage or special virtue in submission. He looks upon it as an act of folly and its perpetrators as nincompoops. It is so that we often look at Calvary, as a victory only, a victory over death, but forget that that victory was won by submission to death. The meaning of this will become increasingly clear to us, as it did to Peter, while we watch with him the progress of the drama.

It was this thought of the lamb of Isaiah's prophecy that first suggested to Peter a sacrificial significance in the attitude of men to Jesus and the result of that attitude. This sacrificial aspect was to force itself upon him many times during that first Good Friday, but it was not to yield up fully the secret of its meaning until Jesus Himself explained it during the forty days between His Resurrection and Ascension.

To Peter as to all Jews, the sacrificial system was part and parcel of his life. Religion was not then, as now, put aside in a special compartment to be brought into action once a week. True the Sabbath was held in reverence, but the Temple was open daily and all the services therein referred continually to the efficacy of sacrifice to God for the forgiveness of sins. The portions of scripture which had just occurred to Peter's mind were passages with which he was very familiar through hearing them often read in the local synagogue services, and they provoked further thought upon the sacrificial services themselves.

But this was a line of thought which wearied an already weary Peter if he continued in it too long. It was involved, and it had no precedent except in the writings of the prophets themselves. He had arrived at one clear conception which might, he thought, prove to have some truth in it—if Calvary was a sacrifice as were the occasional services of the Temple, then Jesus was a victim and the Cross an altar. But who were the priests at this sacrificial service? Were not the priests behind the death of Jesus?

Here Peter gave up the involved thought and turned to present events. If Peter kept silent during the whole of the Calvary scene it must only have been due to his thinking occupying all his mind. It is difficult to believe that a man of his temperament would keep silent, it would be too untrue to his character, for even if his own sense of shame and self-contempt, caused by his disloyalty to Jesus, made him feel a poor sort of champion for the Master, yet his own impetuosity must have compelled him to speak his mind about those around him. That he did so we have no proof. In the Gospel according to Mark, which he influenced, there is no mention of any protest or prominent part played by him at Calvary, and in any case it is doubtful if he would have been heard above the shouts and laughter of the mob. But all they said and did to Jesus must have cut him to the quick. How we boil with indignation if someone we love and respect is traduced in company, and if we find ourselves his only champion how impotent we feel.

The Scribes and Pharisees reviled Jesus because they were disappointed in Him, and Peter realized that that was also the real reason behind his own desertion of his Leader. They had expected a certain type of character in the Messiah and He had not lived up to their expectation. But whose fault was that? Surely their own in that they had either purposely or unconsciously misread the clear statements of the prophets, yet they were venting their pent-up wrath of three years, caused by their disappointment, on Him who claimed to be the Messiah. Peter had got one step farther than they. By sane reasoning he was almost convinced that Jesus was right and the rulers of Israel wrong, and his wrath was turned in upon himself for his weak folly.

The Roman soldiers about the Cross too were scoffing at Jesus, but their coarse jests were for another reason. They had no anger against Christ. They blasphemed Him because they held Him in contempt. Had He come in the character expected by the Scribes and Pharisees, decked out in martial trappings, and leading companies of Jewish soldiers, the Romans would have granted Him the respect they always paid a foe. Peter knew that. The fact that His personality had not impressed the martially-minded of His nation and that they had cast Him off was food for uproarious laughter among the legionaries of Rome. Here, too, as he listened to their evil vituperation, Peter found that before he had had much in common with them. The submissive attitude of Christ in the Court-house; His almost negative-appearing personality as it had seemed then to Peter, had roused his ire and, he confessed it to himself, a slight contempt.

There are still these two classes of opponent to Christianity, these two attitudes of mind to Jesus in the world today, and the cause of their respective opposition is the same in our time that it was in the day of Peter; they cannot understand the submission of Jesus. We have already seen that the Apostle had by now received a glimpse of what that submission might mean, but there are many of our contemporaries who have not arrived as yet at an idea of that meaning.

First there are the people who have been reared in Christian homes. From infancy they have been taught about Jesus, and through Sunday-school and Bible Class they have followed the story of His life. All throughout that time He was little more than a historical character in a book to them, and they had come to look upon His chief characteristic as power. It is only a child's way to

look for and expect power in its heroes, and no matter
how the meekness of Jesus was stressed in those early
years, the characteristic of power conveyed in the works
of the Master overshadowed it until it was practically lost.
That is true of child-psychology. Then these young Christians are thrust out into a pagan world, for such we must
truthfully call it, and they begin to realize the amount of
sin it contains, and how powerful the forces of sin really
are. Jesus, they have always associated with power, and
they cannot understand now that the Godhead of Christ
is beginning to dawn upon their minds, how it is if He
is God, that sin has such power. They hear of Jesus again
and again in Church and as they listen they hear the
half-forgotten submissiveness of Jesus being stressed, and
it nearly captures their mind. But the force and power of
sin against the submission of Jesus sounds ridiculous. They
cannot see until they become converted that the submission of Jesus to the evil wills of men was part of the
scheme to destroy the power of evil, and that it needed
greater strength, power, courage, than they themselves
imagine. So gradually they relinquish their faith and
become servants of the enemy.

In the second class are those to whom some reference
has been made before, the people who expect Christ or at
least His Church to be a powerful leader in international
policy. They would admire and give full support to a
'God of battles'; One who would lead victorious armies
of either force or policy against the things contrary to
His liking. The fact that the Church, the Body of Christ
on earth, holds itself aloof, as did Jesus, from such worldly
matters is incomprehensible to them, and being so, is
below their contempt, and they continue in ignorance of
the glorious truth that religion is personal, rather than
national.

The real reason why these two classes of persons give
up following Christ is because they find themselves in the
minority. There has come a point in their lives as it did
in the lives of both Peter and Pilate during the trial of

D

Jesus, when overwhelming odds have been set against them, and they have wavered and fallen rather than face the battery of condemnation. At first they have continued to hold the views inculcated into them in infancy, then they have come up against scoffing and laughter thrown at them for their Christian adherence. Derision of any kind is very hard to bear. We can understand out of our own experience the failure of these two classes of people. But even this experience has not taught them as it would have done if they had thought it all out logically, that it must be a religion of power if it is followed by those who have stood this test in which they themselves have failed.

For instance, how many are there in the world today who, though Christian in their idealism, would not obey their earthly master even if the fulfilling of his command meant unchristian suffering for others, rather than stand by their ideals and run the risk of dismissal from their wage-earning occupation? Such had been Pilate's position when called upon to deliver up Jesus for crucifixion. Would it not have been a powerful belief he had shown if, on the other hand, he had let Him go free and challenged Caesar to do his worst? We know which would have been the more powerful of the two forces from a worldly point of view, but which would have succeeded most in building up character? And that lasts beyond this world.

Pilate's failure to support the claims of Christ, although they had impressed him so much when faced with their exponent, was the result of cowardice, but Peter's denial was the outcome of cowardice of a different kind.

Here let us pause for a moment to see how often we place ourselves in the position of Pilate or Peter at that time of crisis in their lives. We have arrived at that state of mind when the power of the personality of Jesus in all its attractiveness has been revealed to us. We feel that we must submit to His appeal, become followers of Him. The revelation of the character of Christ has been so bright that it has completely blinded us to the present circumstances of our life in which our friends and acquaintances play so large a part. Now the decision to submerge ourselves in the personality of Jesus may mean the loss of many friends to whom He means nothing at all. What are we to do? Keep our friends and lose Jesus, or choose Him and lose our friends? Did not Jesus foresee this position when He spoke of its being necessary to forsake all our former acquaintances if they stand between Him and us, before we attempt to follow Him?

All these thoughts which occur to the conscientious student of life have as their centre the Cross of Calvary. In it is to be found the answer to all the problems with which life confronts us. By it we are to find that 'way of escape' which is promised to the hard-pressed soul.

Let us, through the eyes of Peter, see it as an object of grandeur, not ignominy: the sacrifice of a Person for the individual persons of the whole world. Slowly the glorious truth of this was to dawn upon the Apostle whose fortunes we are following, but it was only by deep spiritual consideration, not taking the event at its face value as do so many, and therefore going away disappointed.

As he gazed, Peter wondered. On that previous occasion Jesus had refused to obey the devil's appeal to cast Himself down from the pinnacle of the Temple. Would he now accede to the demand of His persecutors? The Apostle had not yet cleared his mind as to the exact meaning of the submission though his thoughts on the matter were arranging themselves, and he felt in his heart that Jesus could if He would, come down from the Cross. Yet, when he saw that Jesus took no more heed of the calls to Him from below than He had of the rabble in the council chamber, I do not think Peter was disappointed. To him it would no doubt have appeared incongruous and out of keeping with all that had gone before, as we who look back along the avenue of the centuries know it would have been.

Many of the seeming anachronisms in our religious experience would appear cogently reasonable if we would strive to see them from the point of view of Christ instead of with our own limited, finite mind. Peter was slowly coming to that Christ-viewpoint which was to open up to him a new world of belief.

Peter was now jerked from his musings by a new turn of events in the drama before him. The thieves crucified on either side of Jesus had up to now occupied but little of his attention. Now they suddenly became the focus point of the whole scene. The thief on the left was a vile type of fellow, and there is little doubt but that both he and his comrade in sin had good knowledge of the work and teaching of Jesus. The second thief was of a more reasonable turn of mind. Both had evidently been watching Jesus, each amazed in his own way but for different reasons by the submissive aspect of the victim. At last the viler of the two could keep silence no longer. Anxious for his own escape, he strained at the thongs binding him to his cross, and half in earnest, half in jest, roared out: 'Art Thou the Christ? Save Thyself and us.' What exactly was behind that cry we shall never know, whether it was a glimmering of the truth about Jesus that prompted it, or a last defiant ribaldry on the thief's part before death silenced him for ever. It would appear that his comrade took the latter view, and as he probably knew him very well, it may have been the correct one. However, this second thief was a man of clearer perception and deeper insight than his fellow and seems to have glimpsed the Godhead in Christ in those moments of clear vision before death, for he rebuked the first thief with the words: 'Dost thou not fear God, seeing thou art in the same condemnation? And we indeed justly; for we receive the due reward of our deeds: but this Man hath done nothing amiss.' Then he turned to Jesus with an act of faith which, considering the circumstances and the time of its utterance, was little short of miraculous, and said: 'Lord, remember me when Thou comest into Thy kingdom.'

Let us try to see how miraculous that utterance really was. To the mind of this thief death would be just as final as Peter had thought of it when he first saw Jesus on the Cross. True, since the Psalmist's day there had been a great development in the Jewish conception of the after-life, but it might well have been the conception of the theologians only, not of the ordinary man.

Peter at any rate stood spellbound before such a faith; a faith greater than his own, which called for future succour beyond death, from One who apparently was in a position equally helpless to that of the suppliant. Again Peter felt that flush of shame covering his face. He who was to have been the leader of the chosen Apostles, a child in faith compared with one who had never followed Jesus at all.

But the answer of Jesus from the Cross to the thief plunged Peter still farther into the valley of despondency. 'Verily I say unto thee,' said Jesus, 'today shalt thou be with Me in Paradise.'

First, Simon of Cyrene, a man whom the Apostle did not know, and certainly not a follower of Jesus in the accepted sense of the word, had carried the Cross of Christ, while he, Peter, one of the chosen three and the one who was to be the rock upon which the future Church was to be built, had walked alongside with the deriders of the Master. Now a thief was given the pre-eminence as the first to enter Paradise with the Messiah while Peter, who had vowed loudly never to leave Him, stood at the foot of the Cross with the blasphemers.

How often have those who are earnest Christians and good workers for Christ, when meeting some man, a non-churchgoer, and finding in him some signal aspect of the grace of God, felt just at first a twinge of jealousy that one who is not a follower should show such a reflection of Jesus in his character? Peter felt that twinge of jealousy now as he had felt it when the Negro had carried the Cross. It was a punishment for his first failure to serve fully the will of his Master.

It was not the first, nor was it to be the last indirect rebuke from Calvary to the waiting Apostle. We shall see how more and more it was borne in upon Peter that this drama was a personal matter in which he himself was deeply involved.

FOUR

'Woman, behold thy son; son, behold thy mother'

THE JEERING and the laughter grew more faint and intermittent. The great crowd had tired itself out with its own levity, and people were grouped together talking in low voices. Occasionally a voice would be raised in ribald diatribe against the hanging Christ, but after a while even these individual excursions into open blasphemy failed to rouse any supporting shouts. To Peter it seemed that the silence was not a self-imposed quietness, but as if it were being forced down upon the throng from without; as if some agency were at work quelling men's hearts and minds and voices; as if a slow process of paralysis were setting in. He even noticed in the eyes of some a lurking fear for which they themselves could not as yet account. And low on the far horizon behind the Cross was a small cloud, no bigger than a man's hand, which appeared slowly to approach, so slowly that motion was almost imperceptible, and slowly to grow larger.

It was now that he noticed two familiar figures among those at the foot of the Cross; it was the beloved disciple, John, and Mary, the mother of Jesus. How long they had been there he did not know. At first he felt an impulse to join them, then the memory of his denial in the council chamber swept over him. John would know of that, and though Peter might have faced Jesus after His prayer for the forgiveness of His persecutors, and might have faced John, who always understood so well, he could not face the Mother of his Master. She, too, might know of his fall, and he could not bear to see accusation in those eyes.

The impulse to go forward on recognizing his friends was checked, and instead he moved farther back until there were two or three people between himself and recognition. So he stood watching in the growing still-ness and, as he watched, the little cloud drew silently nearer, until the wood of the Cross was blended into the dark background, and the figure of Jesus gleamed apparently unsupported in mid-air. The scene in its horror and eeriness caught Peter's breath.

Still Jesus was silent, and in the general stillness Peter continued the sacrificial idea which had already appealed to him. Silent as the lamb before its shearers was the Son of God—the Lamb of God. On either side the two crucified thieves could hardly be seen against the growing darkness.

It was the sight of Jesus between these two thieves which, taken in conjunction with his already forming sacri-ficial idea of Calvary, suggested a corroborative theme to Peter. Was it not the case that these two thieves were dying for sin? It was one of the most primitive and simple laws of man that death should be the penalty for sin or the breaking of a law, in order that people might be deterred from sin. Could it not then be argued that these two thieves who died for sin were dying for the people to save them from committing sin? It was almost as if these two were a sacrifice at the hands of the law to improve the citizenship of the people. And was it not true that in the Jewish sacrificial services the priest stood between the severed halves of the sacrificed animal, thus uniting himself with the sacrifice? As Peter looked upon Christ hanging between the two thieves, the thought occurred to him: 'Was Jesus then a priest as well as a victim? Was He not uniting Himself with the sinners of the world as represented by the thieves, just as the Jewish High Priest united himself with the sins of the people as represented by the sacrificed animal?' The thought opened up tremendous possibilities, and Peter was astounded by the enormity of his discovery, if discovery it was!

Of course Peter was not sure as yet if Jesus was a

sacrifice—never mind a priest—in some higher sense and meaning of the words than mankind yet understood. Complete conviction was to come later. But once this sacrificial idea had suggested itself to him, another incident in the life of the Master fell into its place and yielded up its meaning. Was not one of the sacrificial services the putting upon the sacrificial animal the sins of the people by the imposition of the hands of the priest, and the driving out of the animal into the wilderness? And had not Jesus, immediately after the descent of the Holy Spirit upon Him, felt Himself driven forth into the wilderness? 'The goat for Azazel'; the phrase sprang into his mind. And now a new and more terrible significance was given to those Forty Days, and Temptation in the Wilderness—the place of the evil forces and the lord of darkness.

A new world was opening up before the mind of the Apostle; a world of new values, a place of symbols, where every aspect of life had its spiritual parallel, good or evil; and where man could no longer look upon his actions as things of the moment, but must realize in them forces for eternity to the good or ill of his individual soul, and saving or damning of the souls of others with whom he came into daily contact. Peter thought of his denial in the light of that faint, indistinct knowledge which was slowly dawning upon him, and his heart sank at the newly realized enormity of his offence. Would not others —weaker than he—have taken heart if he had stood out boldly for Jesus until the end; and had even died with Him? Peter was learning—as all followers of Jesus must eventually learn—that 'no man liveth unto himself, and no man dieth unto himself'.

The cloud—now shaped like a large fan with its point on the distant horizon—appeared to have ceased its slow progress, and the semi-twilight it caused subdued the bizarre colours of the people's robes. They themselves were under the same subduing influence and some—the weaker ones—quietly slipped away from the crowd, and made their way down into the city at the foot of the hill.

Jerusalem was still under the white glare of the afternoon sun; the cloud had not yet cast its pall upon it and from its streets came the murmur of talk and traffic, and the laughter of its children, throwing into greater relief the stillness round the Cross.

Peter felt a spirit of foreboding was abroad. Before this new idea of a wider life of the spirit, in the days when he was worldly, and would have scoffed at such an idea, he would have been terrified by this eerie atmosphere and fled incontinently, as he had done from the council chamber; but now, in his new knowledge, he stood his ground, interested in watching this growing terror—which only their bravery cloaked—falling upon the Roman soldiers who stood on guard.

A worldly man, proud in his self-sufficiency and brave by this world's standards, often proves himself an arrant coward when suddenly up against powers and forces not of this world, which his limited intelligence precludes him from understanding. It is only when he has realized that earthly life is but a small part of the life there is in the universe, and that Jesus is the Lord of all life—seen and unseen—that he can find courage under His banner against the things of darkness.

A sudden light, clicking sound, cutting the stillness, sharply drew Peter's attention. The Roman soldiers— either to increase their courage or to occupy their time— were dicing for the seamless robe of Jesus. Their actions were nervous and jerky, their attitude tense, with often a swift glance upward at the hanging Christ. At last the lot was cast and one of their number stood up, draping the robe over his arm. The others went back to their posts, and the stillness became more oppressive.

People were looking apprehensively at the Cross, and muttering to each other; and moving nervously about until only the sound of rustling robes and the undertone of muttering broke the stillness. The only ones who stood still and did not seem perturbed by any growing nervousness were the Mother of Jesus and the Apostle

John. Peter watched them with a longing in his heart to be with them, to have their equanimity of mind, their clear consciences.

Jesus had lived a strange life, thought Peter, his mind dwelling on the Blessed Virgin. It had been a life of singleness of aim and purpose, and all else had been sacrificed to that aim and purpose. Why, he remembered having heard a story about the Master's childhood, which told that when He was only twelve years old He had remained behind in discussion with the rabbis at Jerusalem, His mother meanwhile 'trekking' to Nazareth, thinking Him to be with the caravan. And when she had missed Him from the company, she and Joseph had returned to the Holy City and found Him in conversation with the learned leaders of the nation.

'Woman, what have I to do with thee?' the Boy had said. 'Wist ye not that I must be about My Father's business?'

In its modern English equivalent, this would mean: 'Mother, to you I am only a Boy, and in your company I am only a Child. Don't you see how much more good I can do for God in learning from the wise?'

Then again there had been the occasion when He was teaching in a house, and His mother had come to speak with Him, and they had told Him.

'Who is My mother?' He had surprisingly asked. 'And looking round on all the assembled company, had said: "Behold My mother and My sisters and My brethren!"'

A final memory came back to Peter in this connexion. It was the Master's 'hard saying' regarding discipleship —that a man must be prepared to leave father, mother, wife, sisters, brothers and even children for His sake and the Gospel's.

Until now all these sayings of Jesus had seemed to Peter hard and unfilial statements, wanting in true feeling towards one who had suffered so much, and was to suffer more for Him. Now they began to fall into their true place in the scheme of things and to appear at their

true and not exaggerated values. Surely He had meant
that discipleship was such an important vocation, and the
gospel He taught of such vital and eternal importance to
the souls of men that anything which deterred a man from
following and teaching by his life or words, must be
avoided even if it meant the severance of such close ties
as those of the family. When mother, father, brother,
sister, wife, or child is a true follower of Jesus, then there
need not be any break; but not even filial or paternal
duty should be allowed to stand between the soul and
God. There was in this teaching of Jesus no reflection
cast upon His own mother. It had been prophesied of
her that a sword should pierce her heart, and she understood all His sayings in the way He meant them. Jesus,
who is the Prince of Love, knew that love contains suffering as an integral part of itself, and this knowledge was
not hid from the Blessed Virgin.

These sayings of Jesus—so apparently harsh at the time
of their utterance—in the changed atmosphere of Calvary,
Peter recognized, had become part and parcel of the rest
of the teaching of the Master: no more strange or puzzling
than any of His sayings. It is a strange and compelling
truth that all the sayings of Jesus, difficult of explanation
when they were spoken, reveal their true meaning only
before the Cross—itself an apparent anachronism, the
death of the Lord of Life.

It is possible because people omit to view the sayings
of Jesus in the light of Calvary that they find them hard
sometimes, and often quite irreconcilable with a religion
of love in our own time. And these sayings about desertion of family for Christ's sake are among the most misunderstood in our day.

The reason for the misunderstanding is in the general
decline of the family attitude towards religion, especially
organized religion, today. Things are not as they were
in times past. Up to half a century ago, religious practice
was common in the family. The children were instructed
in the home about the things of God; family prayers

brought all the family together in corporate worship morning and night; Sunday-school instruction was insisted on by parents for their children, and the family went, as a family, to the church and sat, as a family, during the services. Today matters are far different. Home teaching in prayer and the hearing of the children's prayers by the parents is no longer kept up except in exceptional cases; family prayers are rarely said; the few children out of the bulk of the child population who are sent to Sunday-school are often sent that they may be out of the way—as the parents freely tell you. The Bible is rarely read in the home, and few members of the family are regular in their attendance at the church services. The observance of Mothering Sunday and its teaching may in time correct this fault in family life, but while modern family life remains what it is, it will not fit into Christ's scheme of things.

Now, though things are as they are, the bonds between members of a family remain to a great extent what they have always been. Imagine, then, a modern family such as described in the latter part of the last paragraph. One of the sons becomes converted. Household arrangements for the Sunday must be upset if he is to be able to attend all the services on the Sunday—a true convert's minimum. What happens?

Religion is not at a premium in the eyes of the rest of the family, and he is derided for 'getting religion', as if it were some sort of disease. He is in a minority; all the rest of the family refuse to have their Sunday habits altered in the slightest in order that he might carry out what they consider to be only a foolish whim. If that son is to live up to his convictions, he must forsake mother and father, and brother and sister, for Christ's sake. He will suffer through the breaking of the family bond as much as they will, but with this difference: he will have the compensating companionship of Jesus in his new-found religion, whereas the family—being without God in the world—will have no compensations.

Our sense of values in the materialistic world in which we live, is all wrong. Until we realize the plain fact that nothing counts higher in this life than religious conviction, we will continue to make colossal blunders in our family, our industrial and our national life.

And this is, I think, the opinion which was taking root in the mind of Peter as he watched. Before this time, the all-important fact in the Apostle's life was a national one that Israel should be freed from the oppression of Rome. His religion, even, had been made subservient to that end, and it had been the first cause of his joining under the banner of Jesus, in the hope that He would bring about the realization of that all-important fact. When it had looked as if Jesus was not the Person to do it, Peter had forsaken Him, his national desire being stronger than his love of Christ. Now the reverse was the case; Calvary, fruitful of new ideas, causing him to see life in its true perspective.

So wrapped up was the Apostle in his review of the salient passages in the discourses of his Master that, for the moment, outside happenings were of no account; but the atmosphere forced its personality upon him and brought him out of his study. Personality is the only word that can describe the potent though invisible power that seemed to be abroad as God's Son hung dying on the Cross. Peter felt that it was an antagonistic personality. But was it one personality, he wondered, or a number—all with the same evil intent! His thoughts went back to the terrible trials of Jesus in the wilderness, and he was devout enough in his religion to understand what was meant by the 'Powers of Darkness'. Could it be that they were abroad in this evil hour, when men murdered the Son of God, he wondered. Yet what more potent hour for evil could there be than when men had given themselves up entirely to do the devil's will! Peter shuddered—strong, practical man that he was—at the terrible forces that might at that moment be free to work their will on his Master!

This feeling of an invisible, antagonistic power was to ebb and flow in the mind of Peter during all the terrible scene until, with cataclysmic force at the end, it rent the rocks in its fury at the overwhelming power of the Lord of Light.

With difficulty the Apostle wrenched his mind away from the terrifying atmosphere, and compelled himself to concentrate on the scene before him. The two thieves, stilled as was the multitude by this time, hung gazing from their crosses at the Central Figure. But in the minds of each, thought Peter, the thoughts would be different. There was the thief whose penitence had brought to him revelation and who had been blessed by the promise of Christ's companionship 'through the Valley of the Shadow of Death'. His would be grateful, worshipping thoughts. But what of the other? His mind would be in a whirl of conjecture. The very attitude of Jesus and the calm dignity of His utterance would have impressed him. Did he revile at the end? I do not think so.

Then Peter's eyes rested upon that Central Figure itself. Submissive still, Jesus hung there, His eyes now closed, yet the strong lines of the face showing that His mind worked strenuously still against opposing forces. Peter's eyes closed, too, for he could not bear to look longer on Him whom he had denied, yet whom he loved so well.

John, Peter noticed, had his arm about the shoulders of the mother of Jesus and she, in her weakness, was leaning heavily upon him. Her eyes kept gazing up into the beloved face of her Son; then—her features torn with anguish—her head would fall again upon her breast.

John's eyes were dry, but they held that stony stare which betokens a grief too strong for tears. He never looked up, but straight, unseeingly, in front of him. Was he—as Peter had already done—reviewing all the old lovable scenes of that blessed companionship, the Apostle wondered.

Have you ever watched a loved one suffer and die? If so, you will be able to enter into the tragic minds of John and the Blessed Virgin at this moment—especially if you are a mother. It is as if part of yourself—an integral, vital part—is dying too. The future looms black and forbidding, and hope has fled, as it seems, for ever. True, John and the Mother of Jesus had a clearer perception of all that this dying of their Loved One meant; but even to them —until complete revelation came with the Resurrection of Christ—the present tragedy must have overclouded the future glory.

Whether Peter had any children, we do not know; but as a married man he must have known how, in the family —'if one member suffer all the members suffer with it'. The illness of his wife's mother had no doubt cast a gloom over the whole household until the healing hand of Jesus restored her to health.

So now, as he gazed at John and Mary, must he have been able to enter deeply into their suffering. But what a difference was there between their suffering and his! They, with consciences quite clear, knowing they had done all that could possibly be expected of them, to help Jesus, were concerned only with a personal loss. Peter, on the other hand, faced the terrible situation that he had had a personal hand in this Crucifixion, through his lack of moral courage.

To many, the attitude of John during the trial of Jesus is very puzzling. Why, they ask, since he had influence enough not only to get himself and Peter allowed in to the trial, but was obviously important enough to be allowed in the Inner Council Chamber at that time, did he not exert himself on behalf of the Accused?

But is there really any question to answer? Was he not the Beloved Disciple for the simple reason that, in him, Jesus saw one who fully understood the implications of Messiahship? The Fourth Gospel—which should probably be called the First, for surely it contains a psychological study of the mind of the Christ, which should be studied before we follow the narration of His life in the other three—shows us that John, in some inspired way, *knew* just what the scheme of salvation was and what it entailed. Is it not possible that he realized that Calvary was necessary, and that no human endeavour would deflect the Messiah from the course ordained of old!

In this connexion it is interesting to note that we never hear of any definite jealousy of John's nearness to Jesus on the part of the other disciples. True, Salome, with all a mother's ambition for her children and the current idea of an earthly kingdom firmly fixed in her mind, once pressed the claim of her sons for precedence over their fellows to Jesus. But I do not believe for one moment, after a careful study of the character of John, that he at any rate of the two brothers had part or parcel in that claim. And his response to the query of Jesus, 'I am able,' was definitely meant in a far deeper sense than that of James.

To Peter the Beloved Disciple, in his attitude now before the Cross, would have a greater interest. He would know that John was much closer in mind to Jesus than any of his brother disciples, and watched to see if, from John's attitude—as so often before—he could glean any of the inner meaning of the tragedy being enacted before his eyes. True, the face was averted, and there the most useful key to his thoughts unavailable, but the very tenseness of the disciple's attitude as he stood gazing forward would show Peter how deeply concentrated John was on what he saw before him. The whole picture would be to Peter of deep spiritual significance.

So does the unconverted follower of Christ today look upon the mystics and saints with whom he comes in contact. Here is a difference of outlook from his own on things Christian. The outward show of service-attending and the carrying out of certain Christian duties is here translated into something far deeper and of seeming eternal import. Many do not understand, and condemn the monastic system accordingly. So would Peter have condemned the Beloved Disciple John, had not the whole

E

sacrificial system in all its intricacy already begun to
dawn upon him.

But when the unconverted follower of Christ becomes
converted, when the fullness of the system of salvation at
last dawns upon him, he realizes with a tremendous
amazement that he has till now touched but the hem of
Christ's garment; that up to that point, as it were, he has
but stood on the outer edge of the crowd. Full conversion
brings with it the intimate joy which John knew when
he rested on the bosom of the Beloved Christ.

To Peter this revelation of the fullness of discipleship
was now coming like waves of light beating upon the
stubborn rock of unthinking discipleship.

He watched; and it was no easy matter, with the intoxi-
cating delight of this new revelation fermenting inside his
mind, to stand still. He would fain—but for his sense of
shame in denying his Master—have raced forward and
asked John further to enlighten him as to the final meaning of Calvary. But no—he had forfeited that privilege
by his own cowardice. He must stand and wait, himself
patiently striving to piece together the parts of the puzzle
until the complete picture lay before him.

The thinking Christian, even though he be not fully
converted, can often, through careful thought and prayer,
be guided by the Holy Spirit, as Peter was being guided
now, to the full appreciation of the Christian faith. It is
the thoughtless ones who, satisfied with a partially
observed Sunday, never get further than the edge of
the crowd.

Metaphorically Peter was pressing forward through the
crowd of thoughtless ones, striving with all the reasoning
power of his brain—which was so ably, later, at the first
Pentecost, to build up the logical argument of the Messiahship of Christ—to arrive at the inner circle, peopled as
yet only by the Mother of Jesus and the Beloved Disciple.

The sacrificial aspect of Calvary—that is what holds
that inner circle round Christ together; and it is to that
consummate realization that Peter—plodding Peter—was

relentlessly making his way, with all the dogmatic reasoning of which he was capable.

The midday sun was quite hidden now, he thought; the fringe of the gloom over Calvary was already touching the walls of the city below the hill; a chill was in the air —a chill not consequent on the shutting out of the sun altogether, but as if some horror sought to chill the blood. Slowly, relentlessly, the cloud had grown and Peter— coming out of his mental turmoil for a moment to cognizance of passing events—saw that it was not a cloud such as carried storms of wind and rain. This was no thunder- cloud. It was as if the air itself had taken upon it an opaqueness, closing in upon itself in great folds until no light could penetrate. The sun, he realized now, could still be seen, but it was only a huge brown disk, flat and unreflecting. He had an idea even that he could see the stars—and this in daytime!

He quickly glanced from the pall above to the tragedy below; and a strange sight met his eyes. The gloom had blotted out the figures of the two thieves—only the Body of Jesus gleamed against the uncanny background. The two halves of the sacrifice had been taken away, as it were; only the Priest remained. From His hands, His feet, and His head streams of blood trickled down; a fast- dwindling trickle as the life-force slowly gave way before the forces of death.

Was there a further sign, wondered Peter. Often had Jesus taken the teaching of the Old Testament—Peter's Bible—and filled it with meaning entirely new to His hearers. Sometimes it had seemed that He contradicted that teaching; but always if one thought about it, one could not help but realize that instead He had only fulfilled it—given it its complement—its completeness.

Was He not here doing the same thing in action on the Cross which, before, He had done in words? All the Messianic prophecies He had claimed at the beginning of His ministry were fulfilled—completed in Himself. All these prophecies, as Peter well knew, were based upon the Jewish sacrificial system. Was that sacrificial system not to be superseded, as it were—completed—by Christ's death on the Cross? Peter gazed at the picture before him, steeped now in the symbolism which was forcing itself upon him by the happenings of that day. The thieves could no longer be seen—the symbolic halves of the sacrifice—but Christ, the Priest, still stood out clear, streaming with blood. Priest and Victim! The thought thrust at Peter's consciousness, and he gave way before it.

Was not the Jewish sacrifice made on behalf of the sinner? Then here was Jesus's death translated to a higher sphere than that of political prisoner doomed to die. Here was something which affected the whole Jewish race. Had He not in the first place been condemned to death, indirectly, by the Jewish priests?

Then there forced themselves in again upon Peter the numerous occasions when Jesus had seemed to teach that Jew and Gentile were one in the sight of God the Father. Then this sacrifice was for the sinners of the whole world —a tremendous thought!

Some may feel that I have here attributed to Peter thoughts which he was far from capable of thinking. I do not say that these were clear-cut decisions in Peter's mind. The whole of his thought-process at this time would be extremely hazy, with only a pin-point gleam of certainty lighting up the darkness of his mind occasionally. But his speech before the assembled multitude in Jerusalem on that first Day of Pentecost shows how, by then, he had arranged them all logically.

Here we are but dealing with the first glimmering of a new dawn in his intelligence. Later the full brilliance of the new day was to take its place.

A movement of Jesus's head attracted Peter's attention. Was he again to have an opportunity of catching the eye of the Master and receiving that long-looked-for look of forgiveness? But in the darkness Jesus would have great difficulty in seeing him at all. Peter realized that, and his heart sank again. Still he watched. The lips of Jesus began to move—to form words. What was He saying? Peter strained to hear.

'Woman, behold thy son; son, behold thy mother.'

The arm of John tightened about the shoulders of Mary, and a fresh stab went through the heart of Peter. It was not a stab of jealousy but of unworthiness. First the giant, Simon of Cyrene had come between him and the Master in the carrying of the Cross; then Jesus had prayed His Father to forgive the Roman soldiers who nailed Him to the Cross, but had not looked at Peter—who had denied Him; next, a dying thief had been chosen as His companion through the Valley of the Shadow of Death, and Peter, who now would have died with Him, had been left behind. Now John had been honoured by the care of His mother, while Peter stood in the darkness. It was not the last time he was to be superseded during this grim tragedy, and each time was like a sword thrust in his heart.

'Thou art Peter—and upon this rock I will build My Church.'

The words echoed dully in his brain. What of that rock now? What of that glorious future which Christ had predicted for him?—All had crashed about him in that moment of denial. The sword was to pierce deeper yet, until it had got right under that inner weakness of his— that self-conceit—and levered it out ruthlessly but finally.

The humbling of the conceited must always be ruthless if it is to be final; for self-conceit and personal pride are serpents which continually raise their heads, unless they are crushed under foot. So must Peter suffer in order that this canker at the root of his character be eradicated, and the foundations made more sure.

What is going to happen now?—Peter wonders. How long must this agony of his Blessed Lord go on? Peter in a deep sense was suffering with his Master; to him it seemed hours since that procession had started out from the judgement hall. Yet in reality it had only been an hour and a half. There was still that same length of time to run, and much was to happen on Calvary—and in the heart and mind of Peter—before that last glad cry of Jesus.

So for a moment we leave the disciple standing, and watching, and waiting. . . .

FIVE

'My God, My God, why hast Thou forsaken Me?'

PETER was watching, waiting for he knew not what. It might well be that all the thoughts and half-conclusions that had occurred to him were but the production of a brain fevered by over-excitement. Conjecture after conjecture had crowded in upon him, and, though they might have proceeded the one from the other in a seeming natural sequence—building up what appeared to be a perfectly logical structure of argument—were the foundations sure? As I have pointed out before, his conclusions could hardly be called such: they were so hazy, and the natural corollary to that would be spasmodic doubt of the whole edifice he had constructed in his mind—or was in process of constructing.

So he watched and waited; hoping from the concrete picture before him to fashion fresh theories or add to the fashioning of those already forming. Though the words that Jesus had once spoken about the leaving of father, mother, brother, sister for His sake had, at the time of their utterance, suggested that following Him might lead to the disintegration of the family life, the words He had just spoken gave the original utterance its true value.

'Woman, behold thy son; son, behold thy mother' had explained what was to be the bond linking the family together. The Faith was not to disintegrate the family, but to unite it in stronger bonds. All were to meet in Jesus. When that meeting was impossible within the family, *then* members were to find it outside.

As Peter looked upon Jesus hanging upon His Cross, and at His mother standing with bowed head at His feet, Peter's thoughts went back to the story he had heard about the birth of the Master. It seemed that even at the beginning He had been rejected by men. There had been no room for Him at the inn. That first family group had formed before a manger where oxen fed, with straw for couch and the stars above for ceiling. But it had become a family immediately the Child Jesus had appeared. He was the centre of the family group.

So was He to be the centre of every family, permeating with holiness and fellowship its members. Here in these words just spoken from the Cross was the complement to that seemingly harsh utterance about family severance given during His ministry. Peter pondered upon this in the light of the Fatherhood of God which Jesus had also taught, and the world-wide meaning of the family Jesus had in mind again began to glimmer in his mind.

But if there was the glimmer of a new dawn in the mind of Peter, it was as though the twilight of the world had closed in around him. The darkness had become more oppressive, though as yet it was not black. The spirit of fear was abroad quelling men's hearts and making the few women remaining press closer to the sides of the men for a protection they were far from feeling able to give. Only three persons of the remaining crowd seemed as it were, outside the darkness. John and the Mother of Jesus stood as if unaware of its existence, while Peter was as one apart—a looker-on—watching the effect of this strange phenomenon on those about him.

Natural darkness has always held terrors for the Eastern mind. To those of Peter's day, it was supposed to be peopled with evil spirits, and enchantments were used to safeguard against it. How much more dreaded, then, was this supernatural darkness beneath the full strength of the sun, and how much more potent for evil!

Still gleamed the Body of Jesus; what light there was reflecting on the drops of blood and sweat which covered His poor body—gleamed still alone. Still stood the ancient sacrifice in that Body, like a pale torch in a sin-sickened world. Still did it fill with awe those who gazed upon it and understood not—as it does today those who reject Christianity yet wonder at its power.

Peter saw the immobile Body suspended against the curtain of darkness; he saw the drooping head, and felt that he could even see the straining lungs heaving with agonized breath. That was above him. Around him were faces that gleamed strangely, too—wet with the sweat of fear at the unknown which the darkness represented; cowering almost, yet without the courage to flee before the eyes of others whom they imagined to be less frightened than themselves. Suddenly Peter wondered why he, too, was not like these others; why the Beloved Disciple and the gracious Mary did not cower in fright in this awful hour.

Could it be because the three of them were near to the truth of the matter—the true meaning of Calvary?

He looked again at the dim faces of the people, and he noted that one or two were valiantly striving to overcome their fear. They were muttering to each other, and gained confidence by hearing each other's muted tones. Some even ventured a laugh or a low blasphemy against the Crucified One, but these ended like apologies for having broken the oppressive silence.

Again the Head of Jesus moved and His lips formed words. Heads were strained forward the better to hear what He might say; but no one moved forward. They stood as if rooted to their places.

'Eloi, Eloi, lama sabachthani!'

The cry rang out like the cry of a lost soul in the darkness.

'Eloi, Eloi!' Peter shuddered. 'Elijah!' That was what it sounded like to the startled ear.

There was a gentle rustle among the people. He said something about being forsaken. He had given in that He was an impostor. Now if only He had done that at the trial they might have seen that He was released. The tension caused by the darkness was, for the moment, relieved. One shouted: 'This Man calleth "Elias"!' Another, glad of action after the paralysing silence, rushed forward and put a sponge steeped in vinegar upon a staff, and raised it to the lips of Jesus.

Peter started. Again he had been forestalled. Early in the proceedings, he had seen the bowl of vinegar which was always there at a crucifixion, and had never thought of helping Jesus with the drug. Yet here was one of the blasphemers doing the Master this good turn, though probably in the hope that it would revive Him to speak again. Was he never to be allowed to do something for Jesus?

Then Peter noted that, though the sponge touched the Master's lips, He made no attempt to take advantage of it, and for a moment Peter was humanly glad. Then he rebuked himself for the unwilling thought which jealousy had prompted. He wondered, if he had offered that drug, would Jesus have looked upon him in gratitude. He was almost tempted to try—then the sight of John and Mary reminded him again of his utter unworthiness to do anything further for Him whom he loved so well.

It is an open question whether the sponge of vinegar was offered out of kindness or curiosity. Motives in time of crisis are always difficult to trace. It may have been that the Jew who then approached Jesus was prompted by a sympathetic feeling; or, on the other hand, he may have been prompted by a desire to increase the strength of Jesus, that He might say more.

'Eli, Eli!' The words were being repeated by the crowd. 'Eli—Eli!' Yes, that was it. He was calling upon the dead prophet. He must be raving. That was quite possible. Did not crucified victims often rave in the delirium of agony? They were all talking—the one against the other. The terrors of darkness had momentarily been put to flight, though the darkness itself remained.

'Let be!' shouted a voice above the confused muttering. 'Let us see whether Elias cometh to save Him!'

It was a shout of derision. The old spirit of contempt was creeping back into some of the company, though it was tinged with bravado. But many there were who wondered if such a thing were possible; if Elijah were to appear!

The darkness took on a greater terror to the watchers as they looked about them apprehensively for a possible visitation from the world of the dead.

'Eli—Eli!' The cry rang in their memories. Then some whispered their doubts as to whether it was Elias He had called. Those nearest the Cross were positive it had been God! A shiver went through the crowd. Peter himself—who, like all, had looked for the appearance of the ancient prophet—felt that here was something which sounded nearer to the utterance of the Master than a call for Elias.

'My God, My God, why hast Thou forsaken Me?' With something of a shock, the full import of the words impinged upon Peter's consciousness. Not Elias, but God! Jesus, in whom he was beginning to see One greater than he had imagined, not only a great prophet and leader, but Someone Divine, had cried out to God: 'Why hast Thou forsaken me?'

Many since Peter's day have been grievously puzzled by this cry of Jesus from the Cross. To them, as to Peter, it has suggested a surrender to the belief that Jesus was not what He had claimed to be—the Son of God. There are those today who, taking these words out of their context, have argued from them that Jesus was not Incarnate God, as He proclaimed: 'I and My Father are One' has been set down as the wild claim of One to whom power and success had given a distorted view of self.

Peter was in a quandary. At first it seemed that the whole edifice of his thoughts on the sacrificial aspect of the Cross came tumbling about him in ruins. An unaccepted sacrifice, as Peter well knew from his study of our Old Testament, brought no benefits. From this it would seem that the sacrifice of Jesus on the Cross was nullified in its effects, because of His realization—as it seemed—of the Father's lack of interest in the sacrifice.

But Peter was logical, as has been pointed out before.

Slowly, methodically, he began to review his previous dawning conclusions, to see if the new saying would in any way fit into them.

He was not like so many who, coming for the first time upon an apparent inconsistency in the teaching and life of Jesus, immediately give up their belief and lose interest in their religion. To them it is sufficient that they have met with a difficulty. They will not attempt either to go round, over it or through it. They simply sit down before it, dejected and overcome by an inertia which prevents further effort.

Let us, however, who are so many Peters at this great tragedy of Calvary, like our prototype, tackle the difficulty, and try to see what was the meaning of this strange cry, and what place it takes in the great and eternal meaning of the Crucifixion.

All the previous sayings from the Cross Peter recognized as perfectly normal ones for Jesus to utter. There had been first His prayer to the Father to forgive those who crucified Him; then had come His promise of companionship to the dying thief; the third had been His commission to John to care for His mother. All these three sayings had seemed to Peter in complete accord with the loving, sympathetic Master he knew so well. But the last, 'My God, My God, why hast Thou forsaken Me?' seemed diametrically opposed to the confidence and courage Jesus had always shown. What could it mean? For that it had a meaning beyond the bald surface of its words, Peter was confident. Too often Jesus had shown that His parables and sayings had two meanings: one, the outward, which all His hearers could understand; the other, a deep one which only those who meditated could fathom.

Peter began to apply the method which Jesus had shown in His explanation of the parables to His followers —to puzzle out the inner meaning of these disturbing words.

Of one thing he felt certain: there must be a deep meaning in the Crucifixion itself. He was of too stubborn a nature to give up the reasoning he had already done on the matter, to be baffled immediately by the first difficulty that came along. Tenacity of an idea, which on former occasions had been the cause of Peter's downfall, here stood him in good stead.

Jesus, the Sacrifice for sin! That was where Peter's thoughts had brought him before the last utterance of the Master. At that point for a moment he stayed. The two thieves—symbolic of the two halves of the Jewish sacrifice—had been swallowed up in the darkness and still remained unseen. Alone, Jesus the Priest—the High Priest—hung upon His Cross, combining in Himself with His broken Body and streaming Blood, Victim as well. Priest and Victim! As Victim He was, Peter had reasoned, an offering for the sins of the Jews—but also of the Gentiles. It was upon the 'sin offering'—the 'goat for Azazel'—that the sins of the people were symbolically laid by the imposition of the Priest's hands. It was then driven out into the wilderness, to the Powers of Darkness.

That was something that belonged to the Old Dispensation. Peter was wise enough to realize that in the life and teaching of Jesus—which was a completing of that dispensation—a completing of the Divine Design for the salvation of mankind. Might it not be that the sacrificial system of the Old Dispensation was the story of a parable, and that the Cross was the spiritual significance of it? Here was an avenue which, if explored, might lead to a solution of the riddle set by the amazing cry from the Cross.

We of a later day know how often in sermon and spiritual address, and even in prayers and hymns, this idea is carried out with regard to the Old Testament. Stories are taken from it, and new meanings given to them in the light of the words of Jesus. To Peter, however, this was a new thought and, as such, came with startling vividness into his mind.

He pictured the scene as it had appeared before him on numerous occasions. The animal for the sacrifice restrained with thongs in the Temple until such time as it should be needed to play its part. Then the imposition of the hands of the High Priest, with the mystic words accompanying the release of the animal and its being driven forth into the wilderness to become the prey to all the terrors of that place. It had seemed very inhuman; yet it had been man's way. The animal had no knowledge of the part it played, nor of the grim responsibility which it carried. It had only been a metaphorical burden-carrier for the people. It had no thoughts, no feelings with regard to its sacrificial duties.

But Jesus had taken its place; that was the next step—a logical step—for Peter to take. And Jesus, though He claimed to be the Son of God, was human, the Son of a human mother. Peter could recollect times when He had heard of His fasting in the wilderness; in his own experience of the Master he could remember times when He had been thirsty and tired and sometimes disappointed. If Jesus were really offering Himself as a sacrifice for the sins of Jew and Gentile, then He was taking upon Himself a terrible responsibility of which He would be fully cognizant. Yet Peter could see no other way of accounting for His Crucifixion in the light of His own prophecies regarding it. He had said that He must be 'offered up'; that He must be crucified; and here before Peter was the fulfilment of those prophecies. Was it possible for one human to bear so great a burden as the sins of the world? 'My God, My God, why hast Thou forsaken Me?' was surely a natural corollary to the crushing weight of so grievous a burden upon one's spirit. But that was not all.

The 'Burden-bearer' had been a symbol in the ritual of the Jewish sacrificial services. The fact that each individual one should be a burden-bearer was the real meaning of the 'trespasses' clause in the prayer He had taught His followers. To bear the burdens of one another's sins was to be part of the responsibility of every person who followed Jesus. And here on the Cross He was showing forth in His own Person what the Supreme Burden-bearing was to cost. Peter realized afresh that never had the Master commanded that anything should be done by His followers that He Himself was not prepared to do in a larger way. All His hard sayings—after which many had forsaken Him because they were too hard—He had carried out in His own Person, even to the forsaking of mother and home to obey the Will of God.

A Personal God! Deep down in the inner consciousness of every individual, there is a common hunger for a personal God. It may be covered over with an outward seeming of religious indifference, active atheism, or conventional religious observance. It may even lie dormant and be unknown to the individual, yet, given the occasion and the circumstances, it rises like a cry in the dark:

> *An infant crying in the night: . . .*
> *And with no language but a cry.*

Of what use are the conventional forms of prayer in a time of crisis? How cold and unreasonable they seem. So—to the conventional Christian, the religiously indifferent, and the startled atheist—do words seem when he is up against the realities of life and the grave difficulties of the moment.

The moment comes—the time of crisis—when all one's usual stays and supports seem weak and unreliable; when all help from those we can see and feel fades away, leaving us to face some grave problem or disaster alone—and so alone!

Is there a Personal God, questions the spirit within one—a God who is interested in the difficulties of one weak individual among the teeming masses of humanity? The Bible answers: 'Yes!'

From the very dawn of religion, when the morning stars sang together, and cark and care were as yet not brought forth by a sinning world, God chose out persons, the old chroniclers tell us. God is a Spirit, so that He needed a human tongue with which to speak to human ears; human hands to give comfort and support; human eyes to see the difficulties of His humans and to respond to them with the look of love and understanding; and human feet to carry the human vehicle of His Love and Revelation among the haunts of men.

So through the succeeding ages of Israel's history we see in all times of crisis, when the storms of impending chaos, caused by human folly, were tossing about the world, one individual thrown up on the crest of the wave to dominate the situation, to quiet the storm, to speak the words of rebuke and encouragement with which he had been inspired of God.

God could have continued to thunder from Sinai, continued to show Himself in portentous signs—a column of fire by night, a pillar of cloud by day—but, instead of persisting in such an impersonal method of contact with men, He employed men more and more and signs less and less, consecrated to His purposes, to do His Will among men.

The culmination of this scheme was the Incarnation of His Blessed Son, Jesus Christ. From using other men as the vehicles of His Message, God clothed Himself in manhood and came among His creatures. It was the supreme act of a Personal God, intensely interested in and bound up with the future of each individual of His human creation.

And therein lies the blessed truth which makes life a thing of joy for the converted Christian. The sane, reasonable man wants to be able to worship a God who has faced the realities of life, the facts of human existence; who has faced temptation, disappointment, contempt, social problems—aye, and even death itself: Human death; a God who does not ask of His creatures that which He Himself has not experienced. And the answer to such a sane demand is Christianity.

'He was tempted in all points like as we are, yet without sin.'

Is there any personal problem for which we can require more than the knowledge that our God, as a Person, faced the same Himself; and understands, sympathizes, and encourages us personally to win out against it, as He did!

He will not allow us to be tempted above that we are able, but will, with the temptation, make a way of escape. That way of escape is through personal contact with Him; by prayer, by meditation upon His Word, and by reliance upon His Strength, with the simple faith of a child.

This is the conclusion to which any reasonably-minded student of the Old and New Testament would ultimately come; but for Peter there were only the old chronicles contained in the first part of our Bible, and his personal knowledge of the Life of Jesus, from which to argue. But this final gesture of the Master, this death upon a felon's Cross, was something which Peter felt was bigger than could be expected by the followers of Jesus. He himself, he could remember very clearly, had said, 'Yes, even if I die with Thee, yet will I not deny Thee!'—but it was a very different death which he had vainly challenged; a death less significant, less deep in spiritual import.

The picture which Peter had in his mind of the Annual Day of Atonement was vivid, and filled with horror prompted by the superstitious beliefs of his time. With those we will deal in a moment. For the present let us look with Peter once more at the Central Figure of that terrible scene. Jesus! Ever had He been ready during His Ministry to hear the sorrows and desires of people. The poor people heard Him gladly because He understood their needs so well. In other words, he had always been prepared willingly to bear the sorrows and complaints of men and women. They had come to Him, and virtue had gone out of Him in the granting of their requests. During His lifetime He had been a Burden-bearer for those with whom He came in contact, but to bear sorrows and desires for people was nothing to be compared with bearing their sins. Yet, if Peter's reasoning were right, that was just what the Cross, with its wracked Victim before his eyes, really meant.

The burden-bearer, represented in Jewish ceremonial

by the goat, was a figure of infinite pathos to the large-hearted Peter.

'The goat for Azazel!' The word 'Azazel' itself conjured up a terror of the most horrible kind. Was he not the leader of the evil angels who had been cast out from Heaven for their aggressiveness and sin? And the wilderness was his home. There among the arid rocks and under the blazing sun, Azazel held sway over his legions of evil spirits. It was into this wilderness that the burden-bearing goat was driven after the imposition of the priestly hands. There it would be the prey of evil things. Were there not hairy satyrs in that terrible silence of the wilderness! There, too, Namtar, the Plague-demon had his home; there Lillith, the night-hag, sucked the blood of her sleeping victims; there the evil fiends took the form of jackals, wild-cats, hyenas, to waylay and devour the lost wanderer. The silence of the desert day gave place at night to the laughing, whispering, shrieking spirits. The wilderness was no place for man.

Yet Jesus, he remembered, went forth after His baptism into the wilderness. He had braved its terrors; He had confronted Azazel, face to face, and defeated him there; He had returned from that wilderness—not a gibbering madman as had so many who had got lost there and escaped, but renewed in strength and prepared in soul for His great three years' Ministry. Jesus knew its terrors, Peter argued, yet He had been willing to face the wilderness. Why had He gone there? This had happened before He had done anything of a sacrificial nature for the people, so that here was no parallel with the Day of Atonement service. Yet was there not a link? The goat of sacrifice was an unthinking animal, unaware—as we have already stated—of its attributed function. Jesus was a reasonable being. Might it not be that if He were to be the eventual sacrifice for sin, He must prepare Himself by conflict with evil and conquering it? An animal could not sin; man could. Was it not therefore necessary that He should prove Himself sinless in this manner in order that He might in Himself provide the sinless offering?

Peter tried in thought to put himself in the place of the Master during those Forty Days in the Wilderness. The very thought was terrifying. What manner of Man was this that He could face the concentrated evil of the ages, fasting? A strong man, with all his faculties unimpaired, would not have dared go to that place of evil; yet Jesus, weak from fasting, had gone and won through. It was noticeable, Peter knew, that it was when He was hungry that He had been assailed by Azazel. What strange power He must possess to withstand such forces of evil and, not only that, to conquer them as He had done so often alone in the case of people who were possessed.

Yet, despite all His power—or was it because of it?— He hung there upon the Cross: He bore our sins in His own Body on the Tree. Surely this cry, 'My God, My God, why hast Thou forsaken Me?' was purely to prove to those who came after the full humanity of His nature at that moment. Many there are today who, believing Jesus to be God's Holy Son, feel that their lives are very remote from Him: who, believing Him to be God, forget that He was also man. These in their hour of anguish and sorrow, often the product of bearing others' burdens, feel that God has forsaken them; then that they have failed entirely because of their momentary loss of faith. That is why Jesus—God and Man—knowing the strain of such a burden on weak human nature, uttered that cry through the darkness; that man might know that He understands, sympathizes, and still, in His Human nature, overcomes that momentary weakness.

So we may imagine Peter reasoned. This cry was not a confession of failure, but a cry of victory that He had so successfully combined the two natures in Himself—human and divine.

SIX

'I thirst'

FAR BELOW, beyond the edge of the darkness, Jerusalem lay bathed in sunlight; and faint and far sounded thinly the voices of children at play. Then the pall crept slowly over the Holy City, and muted were the voices; and it lay like a place of the dead.

Again around him Peter sensed a fear among the people. Elias had not appeared. Would God make some sudden demonstration? Their minds, steeped in the tales told round the fires at night by the elders—of God speaking to Moses, and His voice thundering over the cowed heads of their rebellious ancestors—were numbed with apprehension.

Peter himself had lost the momentary panic caused when he first heard those words: 'My God, My God, why hast Thou forsaken Me?' It was all right! It fitted in! The cry of seeming desolation and defeat was really a cry of victory. The Blessed Incarnation was proved by His perfect humanity, in that He, too, had felt that slipping away—as if the Divine Arms had been withdrawn from beneath. He had entered into the very inner recess of the subconscious in man, that withdrawn place of the soul where God and man are one, and in that inner recess He had felt, what every man feels at some time during his earthly life, the slenderness of the thread binding him to God—a thread whose strands seem to part in moments of great crisis.

Here was One in whom man could rest content. His perfect humanity made Him a pattern-book for every facet of human experience and—because of that—an understanding Leader out of every spiritual morass.

In Peter's mind the Body of Jesus seemed to shine against the curtain of darkness.

'I am come a light into the world that whosoever believeth in Me should not abide in darkness.'

The words of Jesus came creeping into Peter's memory. Was that why the darkness did not hold for the Blessed Mary, the devoted St John and himself—that same frightfulness which seemed to appal the people around him? Was this horrible time of enforced contemplation of the Crucified One revealing to him the true view of things? The sea had lost its terrors when the Master had walked to him on the waves; the supernatural had seemed quite natural in the presence of the Master on the Mount of Transfiguration. Come to think of it, it was only on those occasions when a follower—like his impetuous self—said or did something foolish that being in the presence of the Master was anything but encouragingly comfortable.

It was as if Time were standing still—or they were back before Time was, and the darkness of chaos surrounded them. Out of it—out of this tragedy before his eyes—new life was to come. All that had gone before in the history of man had led up to this; from this point nothing could ever happen to man that was not coloured in some way or other by this startling event.

'A light into the world': 'a pillar of fire by night'. God leading the children of Israel out of the darkness of exile into the glorious freedom of the Promised Land, and now surely out of the darkness of ignorance into an age when the Cross would be the touchstone of truth. The thoughts racing confusedly through Peter's mind brought a new light into his eyes. Here was the secret meaning of the word 'Messiah'.

Peter had wondered at times why Jesus was so very harsh to the Pharisees. Might it not be because they had so wilfully misled His people about the meaning of that very word? In their own minds, they had decided just what the Christ would be like when He came; just how He would conduct His mission; what the conclusion of that mission would be. But they were wrong—as is so often the case with those who, in their own opinion, are always right!

These stiff-necked leaders of the Jewish race had read their own interpretations into the Messianic prophecies, despite the spirituality of Amos and the Second Isaiah. They believed that the Christ was to be an earthly leader, cementing the Jews into a formidable people against which the might of Rome would melt as snow before a southern wind. From Jerusalem—His headquarters—He was to rule a world entirely subjugated and ruled over by the Chosen People.

And here He hung upon a Cross, seemingly impotent against the scoffing Pharisees. John the Baptist, thought Peter, must have had a strong inkling of the truth, for he, too, had condemned in no uncertain manner these very men.

Your self-opinionated person always considers himself one of the chosen people of God, before whom the opinions of others are to wilt and wither. It was because their belief pandered to their own possible glorification that the Pharisees were so zealous for it. It was because Jesus stood for the downfall of their beliefs and the consequent frustration of their hopes that they killed Him.

And now—they were frightened. But it was not a case of conscience making cowards. They were not the type to admit their errors. It was plain, stark, primitive fear which lurked at times behind their eyes during the passing of this tragedy. Or so it seemed to Peter, as he watched them.

They, too, possessed all the material which he had used in reasoning so far as he had got. In fact, their knowledge of what is to us the Old Testament, would be expert compared with the simple Peter's. Yet so narrow were their minds and so bigoted their outlook, that no new light could ever break through upon their reasoning until, one by one, they should become as little children and be converted. So like—so very like!—so many of us!

Peter would have been the first to confess that humility had made him mentally receptive to ideas. There had been times during that blessed companionship with Jesus when pride had made his mind as stolid and unrelenting to ideas as the minds of the Pharisees. He had rebuked— had dared to rebuke the Master when He had prophesied this very event in which Peter was now taking part. He was so sure of himself—so sure he was right—that all these ideas which now were his had been rejected proudly. His pride at being a witness on the Mount of Transfiguration had such that he had not realized, even faintly what was dawning vividly upon him now.

When the Master had washed the disciples' feet, Peter had at first refused the service—then gone to the other extreme, instead of just being quietly receptive of an idea of service which, in its highest form, he saw before him now on the awful Cross.

The drops of perspiration that stood on Peter's fore-head were not caused by craven fear—as was the sweat of the watching Pharisees. They were the result of a wholesome shame—a breaking down of the whole character of Peter into its component parts, and a rejection of those parts that did not fit into the pattern of the new thoughts that were rising within him. It was the dawn of Peter's conversion.

Conversion does not mean perfection, but the realization of imperfection. And Peter's greatest fault was moral cowardice. It was this which had withdrawn his support upon the waters of Galilee, and had sapped his courage in the council chamber of Caiaphas. Even the dawning Messiahship of his beloved Master and the indwelling of the Holy Ghost at Pentecost was going to prove insufficient to bolster up his character until the very end. Those who expect conversion—or shall we call it the realization of the reality of Christ?—to work an immediate miracle on the character of the converted would do well to study the life of Peter. There was yet to come the upset of his dispute with St Paul, when moral cowardice led to his

nearly splitting in two the infant Church on the question
of the equality of Jew and Gentile. Although he was now
seeing things eternal in their true perspective through the
Cross, it was to be years before he attained to man's full
stature in Christ.

Let us stand beside him again and watch with him the
further unfolding of the tragedy of Calvary. The eyes of
Christ were closed. The slow weakening of His human
body had cut Peter off, as he thought at the moment,
for ever from the possibility of that forgiving look for
which his soul longed. He had seen the eyes of Jesus rest
upon Simon of Cyrene, upon the penitent thief, upon the
Blessed Mary and St John. But, try as he might, from
the very beginning of that grim procession until now he
had never once been able to engage those understanding
eyes. And now it was too late.

'I thirst!' The words—weak in utterance though they
were—crashed in upon the silence like an accusation, and
jerked Peter from his self-pity to the scene before him.
But he was too late—even if he had possessed the moral
courage necessary. Another was before him once again.
A sponge was being dipped in vinegar, and the man was
fixing it to the head of a lance and reaching it up to those
parched lips. But Peter was resigned in his new-found
humility.

A strange thought suddenly struck him. Never once
during the whole of the Crucifixion had either His mother
or the Beloved Disciple made any move to help that Figure
which hung above them in His extremity. On the two
occasions when His lips had been moistened, others had
done it—and those outsiders, from Peter's point of view.
Why? Could it be that already both knew that all this
was fore-ordained of God, and must go forward?

That John the Beloved was so near to the Mind of
Jesus that he would understand things still hid from the
simple mind of Peter, that disciple was humble enough
to admit to himself. And surely not even John would
understand so deeply as His mother the working of that

unique Mind. A faint recollection began to dawn on
Peter. Had he not heard somewhere that the Blessed
Mary had told someone that an angel—Gabriel, it was
—had told her of His coming Birth. That fitted, too;
for, according to what he had heard, she was still a virgin
at the time, and Isaiah had made mention that so the
Messiah would be born.

Then there was the account given to Peter of the presentation of the Infant Jesus in the Temple. Simeon the
devout had, on that occasion, made a prophecy about
Him: 'A sword shall pierce thine own soul also,' he had
added to His wondering mother. And here before Peter
was the fulfilment of that prophecy.

It was as if that gleaming Body—sheering up into the
covering darkness—was a beacon light for the mind of
Peter, leading him through the darkness of ignorance and
doubt to a full realization of all that scene before him
meant. His pity and love for his dying Master were
turned into an exhilarating feeling of discovery and joy.
Everything uttered by Jesus as He hung upon the Cross
became, in this setting, words of victory. Even now, the
words, 'I thirst,' acclaiming, as did His cry of abandonment, His complete assumption of our human nature,
were a cry of triumph in the ears of Peter.

Later he was to write by the hand of Sylvanus the
scribe: 'Christ also suffered for us, leaving us an example
that ye should follow in His steps: who did not sin, neither
was guile found in His mouth: who, when He was reviled,
reviled not again; when He suffered, He threatened not;
but committed Himself to Him that judgeth righteously:
who in His Own Self bare our sins in His own Body on
the tree, that we, being dead to sins, should live unto
righteousness: by whose stripes ye were healed.' And
later he wrote: 'The elders which are among you I exhort,
who am also an elder, and a witness of the sufferings of
Christ.' This scene of divine agony would leave its mark
on all who saw it, but to Peter it remained always other
than most would remember it. The purpose behind the

event coloured the whole scene. It had to happen: Peter was now convinced of that. Here before him was the culmination of the evolution of the sacrificial idea. Never once during the whole time that Peter had been with Him—nor had earlier followers ever mentioned to him—had Jesus contradicted or disallowed the old law by which the Jewish nation had governed its spiritual life. Here was no contradiction, but a fulfilment and a continuance. In Him as He hung there were gathered up all the Temple sacrifices of the ages, and through Him alone did they receive their full and perfect explanation.

The Temple sacrifices were man's interpretation of how to approach God, and here on the Cross, in the Person of Jesus Christ, was shown to be the one and only channel of approach. Already in the mind of Peter was the dawning of a phrase familiar to all of us as the final phrase of most of our prayers—'Through Jesus Christ our Lord'. The Temple sacrifices were done away—not by contradiction by, but by fusion into the sacrifice of Jesus on Calvary. Peter had come a long way since his humiliation at cock-crow, but he was to travel much farther yet before he attained that grasp of the sacrificial teaching of the Cross so ably shown forth in his two Epistles.

Even now as he watched, and let the mysterious atmosphere of the scene before him flood his receptive mind, another scene from the recent past occurred to him.

Last night—how long, long ago it seemed now!—Jesus had taken bread and broken it, and given it to them, saying, 'Take, eat; this is My Body,' and He had blessed the wine and told them to drink it as it was His Blood. A broken body; poured-out blood—now he realized faintly what this meant—this strange rite that had been enacted in the Upper Room. It was symbolic of what he was now contemplating. And they must go on performing this rite which He had introduced that night.

'This do in remembrance of Me,' He had added.

Other words of Jesus, in a similar vein, began to come back to Peter: 'Unless ye eat the flesh of the Son of Man, and drink His blood, ye have no life in you.' But wait a moment! Was it, then, just symbolic, this rite? Or was the rite, in some mysterious way only known to the Messiah Himself, to be a continuance of the very act before him? When Jesus had spoken those very strange words, many had asked incredulously, 'How can this man give us His flesh to eat?' and they had ceased to follow Him. And to prove that the rite was to be a continuance, and that by it those who took part would really be feeding upon Him, He had refused to budge even slightly from that very literal phrase. Instead, He had turned to the others present and said: 'Will ye also go?'

The meaning that lay behind His words was so vital that He was prepared to lose all His followers rather than water down even a little its meaning.

Peter at the time had not fully understood all that the Master meant—he could not grasp it completely even yet —but his love for Jesus was such that he believed utterly everything that He said. And that was probably true of many of those who still followed Him.

None of the followers of Jesus was a religious leader of his day. They were just plain folk from the congregation. Their theological knowledge was such as would be received by intelligent laymen in the Church today. And one must remember that it is from the ranks of those intelligent laymen that the priesthood is recruited today, as in the time of Jesus. It was not until later that the theologian, Saul, was brought by conversion within the ambit of the Church.

You will note that I said the 'intelligent'—not the 'intellectual'. There is a subtle difference. Peter, like all his brethren, was intelligent, and possessed of that spirit of persistency which, wrongly used, brought him into much trouble from time to time, both during and after the Master's Ministry. But that spirit of persistency was helping him now to hunt down the faint scent of an idea that was to revolutionize all theology and bring consolation to millions of his fellow men.

As the scene before him—of the Crucified One—etched itself upon his mind, he felt that this culminating act also included in it all the sufferings of Jesus. The Temptation in the wilderness; the persecution and insult by so many of the Jews; the agonizing prayer in Gethsemane—surely there, too, His complete humanity was vindicated—and even the misunderstandings of His very followers, were all part of the sacrifice which He was now offering to God. And surely, too, this sacrifice would include the sufferings of all those who, through the long course of Jewish history, had suffered for the faith in God, even up to and including that first martyr for the faith of Christ, John the Baptist.

The sacrifices of the Temple, which Peter had attended for so many years, were all with one object—the redeeming or reuniting of sinful but penitent man with God. Surely this supreme gathering up of all those sacrifices was for the same object, but with this difference: whereas all those former sacrifices had been symbolic, here was the one true, holy, and final sacrifice, made by God Himself for man.

Peter had heard Him claim to be sinless and ask a crowd of people—many of whom had known Him most of His life—'Which of you convicteth Me of sin?' and watched the silent crowd, whose very silence put the seal on that sinlessness. 'Forasmuch as ye know that ye were redeemed . . . with the precious blood of Christ, as of a lamb without blemish and without spot' he was able to write to the Churches of Asia later.

Peter, as he continued to watch, found his mind going a step further. In his anguish he realized that he was as responsible as any present at this scene for the Crucifixion of the Lord. He had denied Him thrice when the opportunity of claiming Him as His Master had been given him. He had misunderstood Jesus all along while companying with Him, except for one brief flash of inspiration when he had said: 'Thou art the Christ.' But even as he had said it, it had taken the form of an anxious question in his mind. The Master's answer he had forgotten in the deep humiliation which almost immediately followed, when he had refused to accept the possible ignominious death prophesied by Jesus for Himself. He realized that all misunderstandings that caused his Lord to suffer, were gathered up in this terrible offering now being made. Was it possible that the sins of man were also gathered up here? His sins were being nailed to the Cross in the Person of Jesus! Here was a personal application which went much deeper than his former generalization.

It was on the Eve of the Feast of the Passover that during the *Kiddush* the Master had taken bread, and broken and blessed it and said: 'This is My Body,' and blessed wine and said, 'This is My Blood.' It was in the setting of the Passover, with all the sacrificial associations that Jesus had inaugurated this prophetic rite. And there in that association, Peter felt, lay some of the meaning behind this strange institution. Their Passover Feast, inaugurated with the slaying of a lamb without blemish, and the sprinkling of its blood upon the wood of their houses, commemorated the winning of their freedom from slavery under the Egyptians. And in this commemoration the lamb without blemish was eaten. So might this feeding upon the sinless Jesus, whose blood was now sprinkled upon the wood of the Cross, stand for the freeing of those who followed Him from the slavery of sin. But surely this new rite went further in its meaning than that of which it was a development. Jews who desired to do so could remain in Egypt and stay in slavery. It was entirely up to the individual. So could those who had heard the teaching of the Master continue in their slavery to sin.

Another thought occurred, too. The Passover had its origin in domestic sacrifices, where every family—or, where families were too small or poor to be able to afford a lamb, groups of families—offered up the spotless lamb. Later, this widespread practice had been stopped by authority, and one central sacrifice had been ordained in their stead, in which all the faithful took part. And here on the Cross was gathered all for which the previous sacrifices had stood—gathered in the Person of Jesus. 'Forasmuch then as Christ hath suffered for us in the flesh,' Peter wrote later in his First Epistle.

But was it just in the flesh that Christ suffered? I wonder, was His brow circled with thorns for the sins of men's minds, His tongue parched for their wayward words, His heart pierced for the wrong emotions of men, His hands and feet wounded for the sins of their flesh? Peter nowhere gives any hint that such thoughts occurred to him; but his insistence on the completeness of the sacrifice would include all this.

The doctrine of the Holy Trinity as we know it had not yet evolved in the minds of the Apostles. That was to await the teaching of Jesus between the Resurrection and the Ascension, and the guidance of the Holy Spirit after Pentecost. The doctrine was inherent in what we call the Old Testament. 'The Spirit of God moved upon the face of the waters', we are told in the Genesis account of Creation. The Jews, when referring to the coming Messiah, spoke of Him as 'the Word of God', and the ancient Jewish writings, when referring to God, use the word '*Memra*' or 'Word'.

But all those books comprising the Old Testament were to remain unedited scrolls for about another hundred years. Then, after careful selection and arrangement, they were to be collected into what we call the Canon of the Old Testament. Co-ordinated study is very difficult from scattered manuscripts, and Peter, having reached the Messiahship of Jesus, could not go that further step which would make him see the Sacrifice before him as Divine in its fullest sense—Very God of Very God torn and bleeding for His sinful creatures.

We must keep the Godhead of Jesus clear before our

minds as we meditate upon His Crucifixion. But the journey which Peter's mind had travelled was a journey possible for anyone such as he, steeped in the law and tradition of his religion.

Some thirty years later, when Peter, by the hand of Mark, was to write his own life of his beloved Master, we note a difference in object in writing it from those written by Matthew and Luke. Whereas Matthew was to give us the Messiah as 'the Son of David and Abraham', and Luke as 'the Son of Adam which was the Son of God', Peter, influencing Mark's account, stresses 'the incarnate, wonder-working Son of God, living and acting amongst men'. And Mark's Gospel, too, gives us a vivid picture of the actions of our Lord, not stressed in other Gospels. It was with the same keen observance that Peter was watching the scene before him, and even now as he watched, his mind was plodding along giving each word, gesture, and incident its due thought and place in the slow revelation which was dawning upon him.

Not yet could he realize the *full* significance of the words 'I thirst!' in the Incarnation idea which he was grasping. They revealed the utter humanity of the Master and, as such a revelation, were of immense value, confirming as they did the idea suggested by His cry of abandonment. But not yet did Peter fully visualize Him who had created the seas, the rivers, the lakes, the running streams, the wells as capable in His utter humanity of crying: 'I thirst!' It was vaguely then in his mind, but time was necessary before it could find its due proportion and place in the scheme of things he was realizing.

There is nothing more mentally tiring than to concentrate for a long period on one line of thought, pursuing corroborative suggestions and hints down the twisting corridors of memory. For over two hours Peter had been following such a logical progression, and it was only the excitement of discovery that counteracted the enervating result of such thinking. We, as we plod along mentally with him, must capture, too, some of that atmosphere of excitement so natural to the soul as it explores the avenue which leads it nearer to God. We have one great advantage over Peter. All that his mind was discovering on this grim day is already known to us in greater or lesser degree. We have, to help us, memories of works read, and the whole of the Bible as our guides.

But the central point of our thinking must ever be the Cross. It stands outside the stream of time and is eternal. Its application is to Cain as he stoops scowling and puzzled over the first murdered man in the history of our race, and casts its redeeming shadow over the last to sin before the curtain comes down finally upon humanity.

As Peter watched he was no longer in Time as we know it, but caught up into eternity so that, human and finite though his thinking might be, yet his mind was led from truth to truth unerringly. In contemplation of the Crucified One, all can step outside of Time and be caught up revealingly in the Eternal.

SEVEN

'It is finished'

ONCE AGAIN the crowd was beginning to get restless. 'I thirst!' had to them been a further confession of weakness and complaint. The darkness was oppressive and frightening.

'And darkness was upon the face of the deep'—the words from the official account of the Creation of the World as handed down through innumerable generations of Jews came to Peter's mind as he looked round in the spreading gloom. The same thought had occurred to him before, but now with a new significance. It was as if once again there was chaos, and God was about to begin the work of Creation. The Cross, then, was an end and a beginning! The first Creation had brought forth the kingdom of the world. Material things had been produced and the final creation had been man.

'My Kingdom is not of this world,' Jesus had told His followers. Was the new Creation then to be the Kingdom of the Spirit?

There was a further parallel, too, Peter felt. In the old account, he remembered, it told how 'the Spirit of God moved upon the face of the waters'. And had not the Master in one of His last discourses before this dreadful day told them: 'The Comforter which is the Holy Ghost, whom My Father will send in My name, He shall teach you all things, and bring all things to your remembrance, whatsoever I have told you.' Again the work of the Spirit was to follow the chaotic darkness.

Man, whose creation had perfected the material world, had soon been at enmity with God through disobedience. Was the new man of this new Creation to be spiritual man?

G

All this was getting rather involved for the simple Peter and, in his plodding way, he sought another and easier approach to his problem.

Man must have been perfect when he was first created; for God—who is perfect—could not make anything that was not perfect. But then it seemed, from the history of the human race which he had read in our Old Testament, man had been given the power of choice. He could remain perfect, or he could refuse to remain perfect. It was most obvious in these accounts and in his own experience that man had chosen the latter alternative. From time to time man had repented of his disobedience and had been accepted again by God. But, except in rare individual cases, this reunion with God had not lasted long. And today the Chosen People, Peter had to admit to himself, were as far from the spiritual ideals laid down by God's inspired writers as it was possible to be. Their materialistic conception of the Messiah's mission was a case in point. Yes, man had definitely got farther and farther away from that perfection given to him at his creation. Then, he must really have been at one with God in this perfection. But disobedience of God's Will had soon destroyed that unity. In fact, man had travelled so far now from the Way of God, that Peter was doubtful if he could ever get back to Him without some sort of help.

A story told by Jesus came into Peter's mind, and here it is as it was afterwards written down by Mark on Peter's evidence:

'A certain man planted a vineyard, and set a hedge about it, and digged a place for the wine-fat, and built a tower, and let it out to husbandmen, and went into a far country. And at the season he sent to the husbandmen a servant, that he might receive from the husbandmen of the fruit of the vineyard. And they caught him and beat him and sent him away empty. And again he sent unto them another servant; and at him they cast stones and wounded him in the head, and sent him away shamefully handled. And again he sent another, and him they killed, and many others: beating some and killing some. Having yet therefore one son, his well-beloved, he sent him also unto them, saying: "They will reverence my son." But those husbandmen said among themselves: "This is the heir; come, let us kill him, and the inheritance shall be ours." And they took him and killed him, and cast him out of the vineyard.'

And Peter's account is followed immediately by that saying of our Lord's: 'The stone which the builders rejected is become the head of the corner.'

It was one of the most obvious of the parables in its meaning that Peter could ever remember Jesus telling. At least it seemed obvious now, in the light of the tragedy in which he was taking part. Here was the well-beloved Son of God—Peter was confident in this belief now—killed by the descendants of those who had beaten and stoned and shamefully used the prophets or servants whom God had sent before Jesus came. And now the Son had been rejected—much as builders might reject a stone which did not seem to fit into their plan. But that stone was to become the keystone of the building. The whole plan of those builders would have to be altered to make it fit. Their earthly, materialistic plan for mankind, with its ingredients of pride, hypocrisy, and foolishness, would have to be pulled down ruthlessly and, starting with the keystone—Christ—would have to be builded anew into a spiritual plan. The Cross must then mark the end of one creation and the beginning of another.

What particular doctrine of Jesus was to be this keystone from which the whole spiritual edifice would spring? That was the next question. And Peter felt himself being drawn through the labyrinth of his previous confused thinking, into the very centre of all spiritual thought and life. If only he could get to that centre and comprehend it fully, he felt that every thought on which he had dwelt during this horrible time would fit into its proper place, and the complete picture would be his.

Surely—and this was important—there must be some

sort of link between the spiritual and the material worlds
if the former was to draw the latter into it and transmute
it into the things of God. If the two worlds of spirit and
of matter were to continue independently side by side,
then they would never meet and intermingle—man would
be compelled to live an entirely materialistic existence or
an entirely spiritual existence—both of which were impossible in a world constituted as ours. Peter could not
but realize through his lifelong teaching and his own
experience that man is by nature a spiritual creature—
a compound of spirit and matter, soul and body. He had
not yet come to a full realization of that conflict so ably
described later by St Paul: 'The good that I would I do
not: the evil that I would not that I practise: O wretched
man that I am, who will deliver me from the body of
this death!'

Here another previous thought seemed to slip into
place. Jesus had claimed to be sinless; and none who
heard that claim made had been able to dispute it. From
that thought, Peter had drawn the comparison between
the sinless offering of Christ and the offering of the lamb
without blemish. But—unlike the lamb—Jesus was without blemish in soul as well as in body. Here was the link
between the world of matter and the world of spirit—in
Jesus the two were at one, and He was, as well, at one
with God. Yes, there must be a triple unity, and Jesus
supplied it.

But how was that unity to be perpetuated? As this
thought crept puzzling into Peter's mind, his Master spoke
again from the Cross of Sacrifice: 'It is finished.' For a
moment the finality of the phrase stunned the introspective
Peter. Every word of Jesus must have a meaning. That
had been one of the wonders of His personality—you
simply had to give your whole attention to every word
He spoke if you were to understand Him fully. And the
meaning of this phrase was not long hid from the Apostle.
The Sacrifice of the Cross was over, and Jesus had succeeded in uniting the spiritual and material in one, and

offering it as a pure sacrifice on man's behalf. That must be the meaning of the words. Yet for all Peter's joy at the thought that the sufferings of his Master were over, there was a sadness, too, in the reflection that they were the last words he would ever hear Jesus speak. For so he thought them. That voice which had thrilled him every time he had heard it, even in rebuke, was stilled for ever, he imagined. And yet he felt it had to be.

His mind swung back again as he gazed upon the expiring body of his Lord. Here was the perfect offering of soul and body, matter and spirit. Although, as I have already said, Peter had not yet come to the full realization of the conflict between the two, described by St Paul, yet it was impossible that in his fallible humanity he should have completely escaped a glimmering of this truth —the spirit and the flesh are so often at variance in all of us. In greater or less degree, 'Dr Jekyll and Mr Hyde' is a true picture of humanity.

This dual personality of which you yourself must be conscious is the ever-present reminder that we are born in sin—more prone to sin than to righteousness. That dual personality was caused by the first, or original, sin or act of disobedience to the Divine Will, in human history. From then onward, instead of man living in one world of spirit and spirit-controlled matter, his every act of sin or disobedience split that world into two worlds— one in unity with God and the things of God, and the other contrary to the Will of God. Man in his good moments dwelt in the world of the spirit, and in his bad moments dwelt in the world of godlessness. While the introduction of sin and the consequent splitting of human personality was and is sometimes nearly completely overcome, so that we say, 'So-and-so is a saint'—and say it kindly—another consequence was that there were and are those who live only in the world of matter, and are completely divorced from the things of God.

This has a modern application even among church-going people. For every one who prays to God daily, and strives earnestly to live a unified life of the spirit, there are literally thousands in our land who feel that a rare visit to a church service is all that can be expected of them. And there are thousands more who never give God, or the things of God, a single thought from year end to year end.

But Jesus, by His very life of complete sinlessness of soul and body, had at last—after the lapse of thousands of years since that first splitting of life by sin—brought matter and spirit to a unity it had not possessed since shortly after Creation. And this newly-won unity He was offering up to God on the Cross. Man, in Christ, was once more at one with God. 'Through Jesus Christ'—the phrase occurred again naturally to Peter. He remembered suddenly a pregnant saying of Jesus: 'I am the Way, the Truth and the Life; no man cometh unto the Father but by Me.'

Yes, it was obvious that the link between the spiritual and the material was to be this sacrifice on Calvary. The sinless way of life had been shown by Jesus; the truth in all its clearness had been taught by Him; human life had been caught up by Him to the plane on which it should always have been lived. Peter, whose grasp of the essential theology of the Cross by his first Pentecostal sermon was to amaze people into conversion, already saw the framework into which he was going to pour that talk taking shape.

But what of the future? Tomorrow was the Sabbath, and the Jews would take away the Body of Jesus; and in all probability the Cross, too, would be removed. All that would remain would be a bleak, unpeopled hilltop. How was this event of the supreme unity of God and total man to be perpetuated! True, it could—and would—be talked about. Peter had already made up his mind about that. And there would be others—John, for instance—who, Peter was sure, would have an even firmer grasp of the essentials of this mystery than himself. They would not keep quiet about what they had learned, if he knew them aright.

So far, so good; but talking about it—excellent though the results may be—would not grip the permanent imagination of people. The prophets had talked, and few of them had been listened to intelligently. The Temple sacrifices had been nothing but mere formalities for a long time now, except in the case of the very few devout.

The Temple sacrifices—but Peter had already concluded that all these sacrifices had been caught up into and interpreted afresh by this Sacrifice of his Master on the Cross. 'Unless ye shall eat the Flesh of the Son of Man, and drink His Blood, ye have no life in you.' And what else did Peter remember Jesus saying about 'life'? 'I am come that they might have life and that they might have it more abundantly.' And the only way to obtain that full, abundant life of the spirit and the body which housed it was by partaking of the Body and Blood of Jesus. 'This is a hard saying,' many had said, and forsaken Him. Yet that desertion had only resulted in a reassertion by Jesus of this key doctrine. 'This is My Body; this is My Blood'—the words came as a natural association of ideas to the mind of Peter. Here was a mystery—the key mystery, Peter felt. Let us enter into the Apostle's mind and go back with him over his long friendship with Jesus as he tries to remember and dwell upon every word which the Master uttered in this connexion.

First, however, let us rid ourselves of all preconceived ideas which we might have of the meaning of these sacred words, right though those notions may seem to us to be. Let us put ourselves completely in the place of Peter, as we have tried to do all through these meditations up to now, and look into this matter with his fresh and unclouded mind. Afterwards we can compare these preconceived notions of ours with the results of our meditations. There is something invigorating in coming thus freshly to a study of some already accepted doctrine, and a feeling of satisfaction at the end of the study.

To begin with, I cannot help but think that this

mysterious doctrine of the Master would be a constant
topic of meditative conversation among His followers.
The parables He always was ready to explain to them
in painstaking detail that they should understand them
and their implication fully. But never once before His
Crucifixion did He ever give even an explanatory hint
as to what these words of His about eating His Body and
drinking His Blood might mean. It would be but natural
then for them to repeat His Words in conversation, and
discuss their possible meaning. Yet not one of them ever
repeated the question of those who found it 'a hard saying'—'How can this Man give us His flesh to eat?' At
least they did not repeat it to Jesus, though that must
have been the eternal query in their minds. They must
have been content to wait, puzzling the while as to a
possible explanation. The impetuous Peter even, who
might have been expected to court rebuke by speaking
his mind, was silent on this point.

Thinking the matter over now, Peter was amazed at
what a lot Jesus had said on the matter. True, he, Peter,
had not heard it all from the lips of Jesus Himself, but
John had, and always seemed to attach deep significance
to these difficult sayings.

It started with the miracle of the feeding of the five
thousand, when the Master had quite nonplussed His
followers by saying: 'Give ye them to eat.' They could
not do anything themselves in the matter, and had to
rely on Him to satisfy the multitude. Peter had realized
the lesson of that at the time. The next day, however,
these same people had come clamouring to Jesus again.
John had been one of the disciples with the Master at
the time, and had afterwards told the others all that was
said and done. Jesus had rebuked the multitude: 'Verily,
verily, I say unto you, Ye seek Me not because ye saw
the miracle, but because ye did eat of the loaves, and
were filled. Labour not for the meat that perisheth, but
for that meat which endureth unto everlasting life, which
the Son of Man shall give unto you: for Him hath God

the Father sealed.' Their minds switched to the miracle by what Jesus had just said, they immediately wanted the power to copy Him in this. 'What shall we do, that we might work the works of God?' they asked. Jesus answered them: 'This is the work of God, that ye believe on Him whom He hath sent.' They said therefore unto Him: 'What sign showest Thou then, that we may see, and believe? What dost Thou work? Our fathers did eat manna in the desert; as it is written: "He gave them bread from Heaven to eat." ' Then Jesus said unto them: 'Verily, verily, I say unto you Moses gave you not that bread from heaven; but My Father giveth you the true bread from heaven. For the bread of God is He that cometh down from heaven, and giveth life unto the world.' And the crowd had replied: 'Lord, evermore give us this bread.' And Jesus answered: 'I am the bread of life; he that cometh to Me shall never hunger; and he that believeth on Me shall never thirst. But I said unto you, That ye also have seen Me and believe not. All that the Father giveth Me shall come to Me; and him that cometh to Me I will in no wise cast out. For I came down from heaven, not to do mine own will, but the Will of Him that sent Me. And this is the Father's Will that sent me, that of all which He hath given Me I should lose nothing, but should raise it up again at the last day. And this is the Will of Him that sent Me, that every one which seeth the Son and believeth on Him may have everlasting life; and I will raise him up at the last day.'

This forthright statement had immediately raised a storm of protest and conjecture among the crowd. 'Is not this Jesus, the son of Joseph,' they said, 'whose father and mother we know? How is it then that he saith: "I came down from Heaven"?'

Jesus answered: 'Murmur not among yourselves. No man can come to Me, except the Father—which hath sent Me—draw him, and I will raise him up at the last day. It is written in the prophets, And they shall all be

taught of God. Every man therefore that hath heard,
and hath learned of the Father, cometh unto Me. Verily,
verily, I say unto you, he that believeth on Me hath
everlasting life. I am that bread of life. Your fathers did
eat manna in the wilderness and are dead. This is the
bread which cometh down from heaven, that a man may
eat thereof and not die. I am the living bread which
came down from heaven: if any man eat of this bread
he shall live for ever; and the bread that I will give is
My flesh, which I will give for the life of the world.'

Disputation again broke out among the crowd. 'How
can this man give us His flesh to eat?' And back came the
immediate reply from Jesus:

'Except ye eat the flesh of the Son of man and drink
His blood ye have no life in you. Whoso eateth My flesh
and drinketh My blood, hath eternal life; and I will raise
him up at the last day. For My flesh is meat indeed and
My blood is drink indeed. He that eateth My flesh, and
drinketh My blood, dwelleth in Me and I in him. As
the living Father hath sent Me, and I live by the Father:
so he that eateth Me, even he shall live by Me. This is
the bread that came down from heaven; not as your
fathers did eat manna and are dead: he that eateth of
this bread shall live for ever.'

Never had Jesus been so direct and yet so deep in His
teaching. After they had talked it over the first time, some
of His disciples, feeling that this doctrine tried them a
little high, came to Him and said, 'This is a hard saying,'
and left Him ever after. But Jesus had not wavered, nor
had He relieved the difficulty of the saying by explaining
it. He had shown openly that, rather than water it down
at all, He was prepared to lose all His followers if they
would not patiently await its meaning by the revelation
of the Cross.

Peter went over these sayings carefully in his mind. It
was a very difficult discourse to understand. The direct-
ness of the words used—'Except ye eat the flesh of the
Son of man and drink His blood, ye have no life in you',

etc., the insistence that His hearers should accept it totally without question, and His refusal to lessen its implication in any way argued that it was of basic importance. Then eventually, at the end of that Ministry, had come the scene in the Upper Room at Jerusalem: 'Take, eat, this is My Body,' Jesus had said. 'Drink, this is My Blood. This do in remembrance of Me.'

And now Peter was standing gazing upon the broken Body and the poured-out Blood of the Master.

Here was the central mystery of the new creation. The Cross *was* to be an end and a beginning—the end of the rule of the things of the flesh, and for the sons of God the beginning of the rule of the Spirit. By making himself at one with Christ, who had made human life one united whole at one with God, man was to be once more at one with the Father. And how else could man make himself completely at one with Jesus but by feeding upon Him, and drawing in His strength to help him in the conquest of the things of the flesh? What mattered the question, 'How can this Man give us His flesh to eat?' Being God and man, He could do all things. The truth of this amazing fact was so patent to Peter and his fellow disciples that 'they continued daily in the breaking of bread'—the first name given to our Communion Service.

The fission caused by sin between God and man, and consequently within man himself between the Spirit and the flesh, was closed by the totally sinless offering of Christ's sinless Soul and Body. And by His divine promise, the repetition of the act in the Upper Room was to perpetuate the union between fallen man and the sinless offering on the Cross. Here was the discovery of a truth that shed such a blinding light in the mind of Peter that it contrasted strangely with the eerie gloom which overcast the scene around him.

EIGHT

'Father, into Thy Hands I commend My spirit'

THE CLIMAX is over. With the words 'It is finished' Jesus has indicated that the sacrificial aspect of this grim scene is ended. Still hangs the pall of darkness over the tragic hilltop; still stands the crowd, though muted now. The whole scene has taken upon itself lately such an atmosphere of eeriness and awe that these people—to whom a crucifixion has so often been a holiday—are compelled to realize that this one has not been as others they have witnessed. 'Thy blood be on us and on our children!' they had cried. Were they now wondering if their idle words, spoken in the excitement of the moment, held more meaning for them than they had ever intended? It may be that what could not touch their spiritual consciousness was having strange repercussions on the strong, superstitious element in their characters.

To Peter, beside whom we have stood during this terrible time and whose mind we have tried to read, the gradual revelation of the meaning of Calvary which has dawned upon him has brought with it that weariness which the exhilaration of discovery so often brings. He has accomplished something, and, the reaction setting in, his mind goes quietly—and possibly tiredly—over the route it has so recently followed. We cannot do better now than trace, with him, once more his path of reasoning.

To begin with, he had looked upon Jesus as a human being—a remarkable human being with strange powers, reminiscent of those described in the old records as being common to great leaders like Moses and Elijah. He had had a very attractive personality, too, stern though He could be at times. Such an amazing human being had He been that Peter, on one never-to-be-forgotten occasion,

had blurted out: 'Thou art the Son of the Living God!'
Such was the power of the personality of Jesus upon him
that he felt compelled to attribute Deity to Him. 'If there
is a God,' his soul seemed to say within him, 'if there is
a God, then this is what I hope He is like!'

The teaching of Jesus, too, had been unlike any religious
teaching Peter had ever had. He spoke with authority
and, what is more, His arguments were unanswerable,
even by the Scribes and Pharisees, who specialized in
argument. True, much of that teaching had been completely beyond Peter's comprehension at the time it was
given. It was only now that it was delivering up its
message to him. Remarkable events and sayings during
that ministry had, up to now, stood out in no sort of
chronological order. The result had been, as we have
seen, to give him a confused if startling picture of a magnetic Personality, intriguing yet always somewhat elusive.
It was only by getting events and sayings in their right
order and viewing the whole in the light of the Cross,
that a comprehensive and comprehensible picture could
be formed.

For much Peter—who had not been an active companion of the Master from the *very* beginning—had to
rely on what others had told him. But those accounts,
given by people of widely different temperaments and
powers of observation, had agreed remarkably.

First there had been the stories told him of the birth
of Jesus, of the Virgin Mother; and these had disposed
him, immediately upon hearing them, to look for further
signs of Messiahship in the Master. But how different
had turned out the reality from the pictures painted for
him by the religious teachers of his time.

Then had come the account given him of the Baptism
of Jesus in Jordan by John the Baptist. Then, accounts
had agreed, God had spoken and claimed Jesus as His
Beloved Son, in whom He was well-pleased. It was as if
God Himself had assumed the priestly function, and laid
His Hand upon the sin-bearer before sending Him out

into the wilderness. How blind he must have been, thought Peter now, not to have realized the meaning of this from the very beginning.

From the lips of Jesus Himself Peter would have heard the account of those terrible forty days in the wilderness— 'the goat for Azazel'—and now, in the light of Calvary, Peter saw this as the first stage in the sacrificial mission of the Messiah.

One of the first acts of the Master, on returning from the wilderness, had been to cleanse the Temple of Jerusalem of those who defiled it with their dishonesty. 'My Father's House' He had called it—not 'our' Father's. The Father had claimed the Son; the Son had claimed the Father in an unique relationship at the very beginning of the ministry.

Throughout that ministry He had maintained that unique relationship with God in all His teaching. 'I and My Father are One'; 'My Father and I work hitherto, and I work.' When He had responded to the disciples' request, 'Lord, teach us to pray,' He had said, 'When ye pray, say "Our Father," ' but in His own relationship with God He always used the words 'My Father'.

Yet we are more fortunate than the simple Peter. We can view the whole of our faith, the preparation of the people for the coming of Christ, so ably portrayed in the whole of the Old Testament. True, Peter had that, too, but our great advantage is that we have also the New Testament, full of the post-Resurrection conclusions of holy men. The whole canvas is before us, and the hands of many expert artists have worked to give us a complete and comprehensive picture of the totality of our faith.

To Peter, the future—which we have limned for us in the New Testament—was all unknown. It was as if he stood—the forces of religious reasoning culled from the Old Testament building up behind him like some huge sea-wave—and looked out across the future, wondering what that irresistible force was going to do to humanity. There, on the crest of the wave, with arms outstretched, hung Jesus like a benediction, whose cleansing presence was to engulf men's souls, and lave and purify them. But in Peter's mind, as he stands between the old world and the new, is a question for which he found the answer by the time he came to preach his Pentecostal sermon. What exactly does this sacrifice of Jesus really mean, and what are to be its repercussions on the spiritual world of men?

The first glimmering of an understanding of Calvary as a sacrifice had come to him as he gazed upon the Body of his Master hanging between the two thieves, like the Jewish High Priest between the severed halves of the Temple sacrifice. Then had come to him the idea of Jesus as both Priest and Victim. For was not He also dying?

From that point the truth had opened before his mental eyes like a flower, and slowly Peter had taken in the beauty and the mystery of it. What, at the beginning of his meditations, had been only confused conjecture was now seen as a whole, the pattern clear and concise.

And as if to round off not only his thoughts, but the very act itself from which they had arisen and which had given them the cohesion and interpretation, came the Master's words:

'Father, into Thy Hands I commend My spirit.'

They fell upon the ears of Peter like a blessing. All the suffering is really over now; the Master is at last free of all that His Sacrifice has cost Him; and in those final words Peter feels that Jesus includes the souls of all sinners, the Apostles' included.

There are still some conjectures puzzling Peter—conjectures that will make him rush impetuously ahead of John into the Tomb on Easter Day. I think he rushed in and was glad when he saw the proofs of the Resurrection of his Lord. Only thus could the whole scheme of salvation be completed.